Digging Up Roots

My Journey to Discover What Lies Beneath

A. Nicole Alexander

iUniverse LLC
Bloomington

DIGGING UP ROOTS
My Journey to Discover What Lies Beneath

iUniverse books may be ordered through booksellers or by contacting:

iUniverse LLC
1663 Liberty Drive
Bloomington, IN 47403
www.iuniverse.com
1-800-Authors (1-800-288-4677)

Because of the dynamic nature of the Internet, any web addresses or links contained in this book may have changed since publication and may no longer be valid. The views expressed in this work are solely those of the author and do not necessarily reflect the views of the publisher, and the publisher hereby disclaims any responsibility for them.

Any people depicted in stock imagery provided by Thinkstock are models, and such images are being used for illustrative purposes only. Certain stock imagery © Thinkstock.

ISBN: 978-1-4917-3386-8 (sc)
ISBN: 978-1-4917-3385-1 (e)

Library of Congress Control Number: 2014908388

Printed in the United States of America.

iUniverse rev. date: 05/13/2014

Dedication

I would like to dedicate this book to anyone that has ever gone through a struggle in life. You are not alone and you can overcome anything with God in your corner!

Acknowledgements

First and foremost, I want to thank God for delivering me and giving me the opportunity to write this book. I give Him all praise and glory for what He has done in my life and I recognize that I am nothing without Him.

To my natural parents, Charles and Marsha Alexander, I thank you for all of your love and support throughout the years. I love you and hope that my future will make you as proud to be my parents as I am to be your daughter.

To my natural family, I love each and every one of you and thank God for all the memories we share and the ways that you've been there for me time and time again.

To my spiritual parents, Pastors Myles and DeLana Rutherford, without your love and sound teaching, this never would've been possible. I appreciate you more than you will ever know for the Godly examples that you are on a consistent basis.

To my family at Worship With Wonders Church, I'm so glad that God connected me with you. I love you all and thank God for how each of you has been a blessing to me. I can't wait to see all the greatness that comes forth from 3WC.

To Jerome and Latunya Dial, Nyanza Duplesis, Anthony Jackson, Leslyn Johnson, and Jacqueline Oduselu, you all have played a significant role in this major milestone. Your support has been paramount from the beginning of this process until now and I can't thank you enough for allowing God to use you to make such a big impact in my life.

And to my two biggest cheerleaders and sounding boards during this writing process and life transformation, Cassandra Williams and LaToya Heard, I couldn't have done this without you! You have been there every step of the way and your encouraging words and bountiful assistance made all the difference. I am forever indebted to you and I pray that for everything you poured into me that God will return it to you one hundred fold. You ladies ROCK!

Table of Contents

Table of Contents

Introduction

You never know what you're going to encounter when you take on the task of digging up a tree. In most cases, the massive size that you see above the ground is no match for the root system that lies beneath. The roots are what keep the tree alive, even when you think you've cut it down. It's the root system that feeds on the nutrients of the soil that it's planted in, literally sucking the life out of the ground and giving it to the tree. It's the roots that can span from several feet to several miles and that hold the tree steady through gusts of wind and other dangerous environmental conditions. For years, I looked at the giant tree that had sprung up in the front yard of my life and wasted time chopping at the trunk and trying to cut off the branches. When I finally got it down to a stump, I thought I was headed towards productivity. The view from my front yard was different and I believed that since I could see more clearly that my work with the tree was done. It wasn't until I tried planting new grass in the yard that I realized that the same tree was still affecting my future plans.

Anything I tried to do had to be altered because I had left that big ugly stump in the middle of my yard. So, I had no other option. If I wanted to have the type of future that I'd dreamt about, I had to dig up the roots.

Okay enough with the metaphorical prose and phrases. No, this is not a book about digging up trees in the literal sense. It is however, the story of how a seed was planted, took root, and grew into over seventeen years of living a lesbian lifestyle. This is the story of my life. Some things will be difficult to read. Some things will be graphic in nature. However, these things are necessary in order to paint the full picture. Maybe you will find yourself and your situation within these pages. Maybe you will find someone you know. Maybe you will just read my words and get an understanding of how these types of things can occur and how to better deal with those who may struggle. Whatever the case may be, I pray that God will use this book to help save someone else, help deliver someone else, and help someone else find their roots, dig them up, and be able to have a clear and prosperous future. This is my testimony!

Chapter 1

The Seed was Planted

No matter the size of any tree, they all start with a seed. The seed is a vessel which contains, protects and aids in distribution of the embryo of the tree to a new destination. It's the seed that holds the identity of the tree and determines its growth potential. This is where the life begins, but in order for a seed to be planted, first conditions have to be conducive and the ground must be disturbed. There has to be a break in the soil that creates a hole, somewhere for the seed to be placed. Once that hole is made and the seed is put in position, it is then covered to protect it and to give it time to grow. The circumstances of my life began to till my ground at a very early age and the seed was put in place as I entered my teenage years.

They say that a lot of children learn the different familial roles while playing house. I can remember the times I played with my cousins as a kid and us taking turns being the different members of a family. Everybody always wanted to be the parents and I couldn't wait until it was my turn to play the mommy just so that I could tell everybody else what to do. We would have pretend dinners together, pretend arguments, pretend school and even pretend church services. We mimicked what we saw from the adults around us and had a lot of fun doing it. But then I got a little older and the new version of house that was taught to me left me questioning so many things and no one was there to give me any answers. My older sister had a boyfriend that frequented our home quite often. So that I would have something to keep me occupied and out of their business, this boyfriend started bringing his little brother around whenever he visited. As this brother and I began to play, I noticed that we were spending more and more time playing games that we would have to abruptly stop as soon as someone entered the room. We would kiss and even lie on top of each other, but nothing prepared me for the game he had in mind on his next visit. He was hiding in the closet in my bedroom and when I went to look for him, he pulled me inside. He had his pants down and that was the first time I'd ever seen a penis. In my sheltered, twelve year old mind I was thinking, *"What's that?"* But before I knew it, he had pulled my skirt up, my panties down and he was rubbing his penis around the edges of my vagina. Everything was happening so fast and I didn't know how to stop it. More importantly, I didn't know if I was even supposed to stop it. Isn't this what's supposed to happen between males and females? I didn't know

anything but something felt so wrong. As he began
to try and penetrate me, he heard someone calling for
us and he immediately stopped what he was doing,
redressed and exited the closet. All I could do was
lay there for a moment by myself, with tears rolling
down my cheeks. I didn't know what to do, but I
knew I couldn't stay in the closet much longer. So I
took a deep breath, got myself up, made sure all my
clothes were back in the right place, left the closet and
pretended nothing had happened.

I went on pretending for the next year but the inner
turmoil I was feeling couldn't be ignored. So many
things about me had changed. My innocence was
gone but no one even noticed. Everything from my
self-image to the way I viewed the rest of the world
had been affected. When I looked in the mirror, I no
longer saw a little girl with platted hair and dreams
of what her life would be like. I saw someone dirty,
unlovable, and unable to escape the nightmare of
reality. With everything I had my heart was crying
out for someone to help me understand, help me cope,
but my lips never parted to utter the words, so that
help never came. It was only a couple of weeks later
that my body started going through all these changes
that I wasn't prepared for and my list of questions kept
getting longer and longer. I was confused because
I'd heard Claire Huxtable talk to Rudy about these
changes being beautiful and part of becoming a
woman. So I wondered why all I felt was ugliness
and shame. I can remember getting the tag line that
my family gave to the girls, "Don't let any boys touch
you, cause you'll get pregnant," but what did that even

mean?! I had more questions than I had answers and it seemed like my little preteen world was spinning out of my control. I didn't know who to reach out to but I knew I couldn't carry this by myself anymore. So I mustered up the courage to tell my secret, but I didn't quite get the responses I was hoping for. The most common thing I heard was to just pray about it and God would handle the rest. Someone else told me it was no big deal, that those things happened all the time, and that I should just get over it. But nothing ever prepared me to be laughed at by members of my own family. At that point, I knew I wasn't going to get the comfort and validation that I needed from my inner circle, so I started looking elsewhere.

Judging from the reactions I got from those closest to me, I made the decision not to speak of what had happened ever again. Since I didn't know how to pray about it, it didn't seem like something that I thought should happen all the time, and I didn't want anyone else laughing at me, I went back to my old coping mechanism of pretending it never took place. This was the summer before I entered into the seventh grade and I figured that once school started I would have more to occupy my thoughts. And boy did I ever! While everyone else in my grade was making connections with peers and establishing their identities, I connected with my science teacher. She was young, we had things in common, and I really looked up to her. She was the only teacher I had that year that I could actually relate to on a level other than just education. She encouraged me, motivated me, and spoke to me in a different manner than any of my other teachers and for the first time in over a year, I was starting to feel comfortable with myself again. I'd stop by her classroom in the morning before school started and help her get set up for the day. She would thank me for the help, but she didn't realize that she was helping me far more than I could ever help her. I was smiling again and when I looked at myself in the mirror I was seeing something other than the nasty aftereffects of one experience. At the end of the day I would go by her room again, help her get things put away, and wait to be picked up from school. This went on for weeks with no problems and no second thoughts, until it got to a point where I couldn't get through the day without seeing her. When I was around her I felt like I could conquer the world, but the feelings of inferiority, fear and emptiness that gripped me when I was away from her were overwhelming. I found it hard to concentrate in my other classes, because I'd sit there wondering what she was doing. My entire day began to center around when I would see her again and she became the topic of all my conversations. The other students started making fun of me and calling me a suck up, teacher's pet, and even a weirdo because my ultimate goal was to make her happy. I didn't understand why they thought what I was doing and how I felt was strange, but the last thing I wanted was to be laughed at or singled out. Once again I was in a situation that I didn't know how to handle, but this time I made the decision not to hold it in. So I wrote my teacher a poem expressing how much I admired her and how she made me feel. I thought it would be received with the same affection in which it was written but I was sadly mistaken. When I arrived at school the

next morning things were very different. Her door
was locked and I received notice from my homeroom
teacher that the principal needed to see me. I walked
down the long hallway to his office with no clue that
the ground underneath me was about to be shaken.
When I arrived, he told me in such a matter of fact
way that my poem had made my teacher extremely
uncomfortable, and as a result, all of my classes had
been transferred to a different team and I was no
longer allowed to be around her. I sat there in shock for
a minute trying to process what he had just told me. I
felt as if someone had flipped the switch to turn off the
oxygen in the room, but I was the only one struggling
to breathe.

What was I supposed to do now? Everything had
changed in the blink of an eye. I walked back down
that same long hallway trying to fight back tears
and wondering how I was supposed to get through
the rest of the year, the rest of the semester, even the
rest of the day without the one person that had given
me the strength to stand up again. When I got to my
new homeroom I sat there trying to think of ways to
apologize and get her to let me back on the team. I
thought if I could just make her understand, then she'd
forgive me and everything could go back to the way
it was before. But how could I make her understand
when I didn't even get what had happened or why? I
knew I wasn't allowed to talk to her, so I figured the
best way to say I was sorry was to put it in a letter.
I took my time and spent a couple of days getting
all my words just right and expressing my deepest
apologies in the best way that I could. When the

words on the paper finally matched the words in my heart I put the letter in her school mailbox and hoped for the best. No harm, right? Wrong! After my teacher turned the letter in to my principal, I was suspended from school later that day. At that point I was so confused I didn't know what to think, but in my heart I felt hurt, rejected and alone. I thought my teacher would have been flattered that I held her in such high regard but it turned into a situation where my feelings were misconstrued and somehow I had become public enemy number one. One would have thought that after facing disciplinary action for having contact with this teacher that I would want to run in the other direction, but for some reason it only made the draw stronger. I knew I was risking getting into trouble, but I just couldn't get through a day without seeing her. I didn't need her to say anything to me or even look my way . . . I just needed to see her. If she was smiling, I could smile. If it seemed like she was in a good mood, I could adjust my attitude to match. She empowered me with just one quick peak into her day. But before long, those quick peaks weren't enough and I needed more. I would find reasons to walk by her classroom in random parts of the day in hopes that one day, she may come out and we'd have a conversation. That day never came, instead, more trouble. Little did I know, she was keeping track of how frequently she saw me on her end of the hallway and I was back in the hot seat. I couldn't explain why I needed to see her, partly because I didn't understand it myself, so another suspension was handed down. I knew after this that things would never be the same. She didn't want me around and I was completely and utterly crushed. The woman who I leaned on for strength, the one that gave me courage and a new will to live and love myself was throwing me away. Feeling the weight of my world crumbling around me, I fell into such a deep depression that my parents thought it would be best if I got some professional help.

A few short weeks later I entered counseling and thought maybe I would finally be able to talk some things through and get some answers to questions I'd had for years. I started with a positive attitude, but after being bounced around to three different counselors and receiving two different diagnoses my outlook began to take a turn for the worst. Then I met him. Before this time, the other therapists I'd seen were all women and offered a certain level of gentleness in our sessions. Even though I didn't feel like we were getting anywhere, I appreciated how they dealt with me. But this man was different. There was no gentleness, in fact, he spoke to me with a harshness as if I was a grown man who had just stepped on his favorite pair of shoes. I wasn't comfortable, but I was tired of being thrown around and having to rehash everything that had happened in the last two years, so I tried to make the most of it. That was until it came time to tell him about what took place with my teacher. I did my best to explain the way I felt about her, that she was someone I admired, emulated and cared for deeply. I went on to tell him how I drew confidence from this woman and how her presence strengthened me. We talked about all the times I'd gotten into trouble for doing things to be around her and then he had an epiphany moment.

He told me that he knew exactly what my problem was and what I needed to do about it. I got so excited at the very thought that someone would be able to give me some insight as to why I had been having certain feelings. I can vividly remember sitting up and moving to the edge of my seat in anticipation of him finishing his statement and helping me in a way that no one else had been able to before. Then he said it. "I feel like your life would be easier if you just accepted the fact that you're a lesbian and moved on."

What was that? Was that the insight I was supposed to get from counseling? Was that the answer that I had been in search of for two years? Would my life be easier if I just accepted that and moved on? But accepted what exactly? I'd heard that word before but I wasn't quite sure what it even meant. How was that supposed to solve my problem? It seemed like in a moment's time I was left with even more confusion than in the years prior. But, he was the professional. He was the grown up. I was just a teenager and he was the one that had been trained to deal with things like that. I didn't know what it was, but something just didn't sit right with me. I walked out of his office that day and never went back. I didn't care anymore about having to start over with a new counselor. I didn't care about having to tell the story again for the umpteenth time. I walked out and didn't even speak of what had gone on in our session that day. I did everything in my power to forget his words, but I couldn't. No matter what I did to put them out of my mind, they kept creeping back in. It was too late. The damage had already been done. The seed had been planted.

Chapter 2

Watering the Seed

Just because you plant a seed doesn't necessarily mean that you're going to get the harvest of a bountiful tree. There's more that's required to make sure that the seed brings forth life. The interesting part of the process is, once the seed is planted, you don't even see it anymore, but what happens afterwards will determine whether or not any growth will take place. No matter what type of seed you're dealing with, it remains dormant, or inactive until some essential conditions are right for germination. All seeds need water, oxygen, and proper temperature in order to produce. When a seed is exposed to those proper conditions, water and oxygen are taken in through the hard outer layer of the seed and the embryotic cells inside the seed begin to enlarge. Water and oxygen, the key ingredients to life above ground are the same key ingredients to life underneath.

So what did I do with the magical solution that my counselor gave me? I'd like to tell you that I starved the seed, it shriveled up, died and I went on to live happily ever after. But if I had done that, it wouldn't make for a very interesting story now would it? I can tell you that before that session with my counselor, I think I had only heard that "L" word once or twice. But being the studious, yearning-for-knowledge teenager that I was, I wasn't about to let there be a word used to describe me and I didn't know all that I could know about it. So I started my very own personal research project. Whenever I had access to a computer I was looking up what it meant to be a lesbian. It became my main focus and any free time I had was spent gathering whatever information I could find on the subject. One of the first things I read described a lesbian as "a female homosexual". I didn't know what homosexual meant either, so of course I had to look it up as well. That search led me to the definition, "someone who practices homosexuality". At that point I felt a little like I was chasing a white rabbit down a rabbit hole, but I was determined to find the answer to my initial inquiry. So once again I headed back to the reference material and looked up the word homosexuality, and this time I finally got some more direct information: "A sexual attraction to persons of the same sex". Then I felt like I was getting somewhere. But wait a minute. Why would my counselor think that I had a sexual attraction to another female? The only things that we had ever discussed that had anything to do with sex were the things that happened to me when I was twelve years old with the boy in the closet. What did that have to

13

do with me possibly being a lesbian? I started to feel
that all too familiar feeling of confusion coming upon
me again, so I knew that I had to dig a little deeper
to get some clarity. I wasn't giving up. I wanted some
answers and I refused to stop until I found what I was
looking for.

A few days after that I walked into the school library
with my eighth grade class and we were given some
free time to find books of interest to us. I got on the
computer and began to see if there were any about
being a lesbian in our little media center, and to my
surprise, there was one. I couldn't help but get excited
but I knew I had to find a few other books on different
topics so that people wouldn't look at me funny. I
went to the counter, got all of my books checked
out and spent the rest of the day anxiously waiting
to get home so that I could crack open the one that
interested me the most. The hours crept by so slowly
it seemed like time was working backwards, but the
last bell finally rang and it was time to go. My heart
was beating so fast I couldn't even wait until I got
home. I went and sat on the bench outside the school
where I normally waited to be picked up, pulled the
book out of my backpack, and I started reading. The
story was told beautifully, about a girl around my age
who was questioning her sexuality. She wondered
why all the girls around her were going crazy over
boys and make-up but all she wanted to do was spend
time with her best friend. The book described the
feelings she had for this friend and as I read through
the pages I began to see some similarities between
her feelings and how I felt about my teacher the year

before. I hated to have to close the book when my ride came, but as soon as I got home, I dug right back in. I had to see what else the character was feeling and if it compared at all to me. The more I read the more I saw a familiar scene and I started to believe that my counselor may have been right. That was until I got to the chapter where the character kissed her best friend. Up until that point the book centered on how happy the girl was just being in the same room with her friend. How the friend made her smile when she smiled. How the simple gesture of a hug would brighten her day and overwhelm her with feelings of love and contentment. All of the things I had experienced with my teacher, but never once had I imagined kissing her. The book went on to describe their first intimate experience together and although I was intrigued, it was a scene that I wouldn't have pictured in my wildest dream. I put the book down and thought to myself that if that was what it meant to be a lesbian, then it definitely was not me. Pushing the book to the side, I went on to finish my homework and do some other things but I just couldn't get that scene out of my head. The more I tried to forget it, the more I wanted to read it again. I justified it by telling myself that I couldn't start a book and not finish it. I had to see how the story played out. So, before I went to sleep that night, I picked the book up again, reread about their experience, and kept reading until I had finished it entirely. I thought my curiosity would have been satisfied after that, but it was just a spark that ignited a roaring flame. I spent time rereading about the girls' intimate encounter every day until it was time to return my collection of books to the media center. By that time, I was no longer just reading words on a page. I had begun to imagine the two girls touching and kissing each other and wondered what it must have felt like. Even though I never checked the book out again, I would still stop by the media center a few times a week and stay just long enough to read the passage and play it out in my head. I didn't understand why I kept going back but I felt drawn to the pages of that book and I couldn't stay away.

The more I read the story, the more I wanted to, but before long it wasn't enough just to read about what had happened between those two girls and picture it in my head. I wanted to actually see two females in action. I wanted to bring life to what my mind had been imagining for weeks. I knew I wouldn't be able to look anything up at school so I devised a plan for when I got home. I recalled flipping through TV channels and coming to 98 and 99, what the TV Guide called the Playboy and Spice channels. Before, there was no way to see what was going on through the colorful, squiggly lines on the screen, but by the sounds that I heard I knew it was something sex related. I sat there wondering if there was a way that I could remove those lines and view what they were doing, then I remembered the cable box that my family had just had installed. This box was connected to the television in the family room and allowed us to get movie channels that weren't available on any of our other TVs. I thought to myself, "*how perfect is that?*" I would just wait until everyone went to sleep and I'd hook the box up in my room. Surely that would make it possible to watch at least one

of the channels and maybe then I could finally see
what I wanted to see. So I went home with this in
mind and it seemed like it took forever and a day
for night to come. I couldn't put my plan into action
until everyone was asleep, but once again it was as
if time was standing still. I tried focusing on other
things but my excitement and eagerness to get things
rolling made the waiting game nearly unbearable.
Finally, I decided that I would just turn in early and
set an alarm to wake myself up after a time when I
knew everyone would be in bed. That way I wouldn't
have to deal with the agony of waiting and I would be
rested enough to stay up as long as I wanted. So, I did
just that.

By the time my alarm sounded, the lights were off in
the entire house and all was quiet. Like a stealth agent
in a Bond movie, I went downstairs to fetch the magic
box and returned to my room with it in hand. I closed
the door, hooked the box up to my little TV and sat
on the bed with a level of anticipation higher than the
moon that lit the night sky. I started on channel 98 and
low and behold the colorful, squiggly lines weren't
blocking the picture anymore. This time I could see
the screen clearly and see that the woman in front of
the camera was completely naked. Other than my own
and diagrams in a book, this was my first time seeing
a naked body, but strangely enough, that didn't really
interest me. All this woman was doing was posing
in front of the camera and I wanted to see more. I
wanted to see some action. So I switched to channel
99 in hopes that it would be a little more entertaining
and worth all the trouble I had gone through. It just so

happened that I turned the channel right in the middle
of a female love scene and my eyes immediately
locked on what I saw in front of me. These women
were beautiful! As I sat there watching them kiss each
other, touch each other, put their mouths in places that
I never thought a mouth would go, I started feeling
sensations that my body had never felt before. I had
taken the bait and I was hooked. I didn't want to look
away, not even for a second. My eyes stayed glued
to the screen until that entire scene was over, then
another one came on and I was glued again. Hours
went by and I didn't move from that spot on my bed.
I sat there watching one scene and after another
throughout the night, paying no attention to the fact
that I had school in the morning. I didn't feel tired in
the least bit, I felt excited. I was completely conscious
and aware of my heart pounding and pumping blood
to every part of my body. I didn't get one moment
of sleep that night but I had this strange feeling of
empowerment that energized me. The only thing that
made me stop watching that channel was the sound of
my parents' morning alarm. I knew that they would
be getting up to prepare for the day, so I had to act
quickly and get the box back downstairs before they
noticed it had been moved. The stealth agent was in
action again and I was able to get everything in place
and back to my room without anyone's knowledge. I
started getting ready for school the same way I always
did, going through my same routine, but something
was different. I didn't realize it then, but through
my very own actions, I was providing the proper
conditions for the cells inside that planted seed to
grow. I walked around school thinking about all the

things I had watched the night before and I couldn't stop smiling. It was real and I had seen it. And for the next few nights following, I continued my covert activities and watched as much of that channel as I possibly could. The draw was even stronger than the pages of the book and I couldn't let a night go by without tuning in. Once again, I was given a taste of something but it wasn't enough . . . I wanted more. I was no longer satisfied just watching the women on the television screen. I had fed enough on seeing the experience of other people. I wanted to experience it myself.

It started out like a game played between me and a female friend of mine. We had already talked about our pasts and I even shared with her what happened with my teacher and what my counselor said my issue was. She started asking me questions to see if I had ever tried certain things and of course my answers were no. At that point, despite my recent reading and TV viewing habits, I was still a pretty sheltered teen. So we began creating scenarios for each other which turned into far more sexual conversations. Before long, those conversations escalated from hypothetical scenarios to talking about what we would do to each other. We came up with code words that we used in place of the different sexual acts between women, so that in case anyone ever overheard they wouldn't be able to decipher what we were talking about. The stage was being set for me to have the experience that I was longing for and everything came to a head on an out of town trip that my church took. She and I had signed up to be roommates but I don't think either one of us knew exactly what was going to take place on that trip. When we got to our destination we went out as a group, saw some of the local attractions and nothing seemed out of the ordinary. Even when it came time to retire to our rooms for the evening we still went on as if our previous conversations had never happened. We were just two friends, sharing a bed . . . like a sleepover. That was until I woke up in the middle of the night and couldn't get back to sleep. We were lying with our backs to each other and I decided to roll over and scoot closer to her. With my body pressed against hers I could feel her waking up but I didn't move. I wanted to see how serious she was about all the things we had talked about, so I waited. If she moved away I would just pretend to be asleep and act as if nothing had happened. But if she stayed where she was then I would know that I could keep going a little further. To my surprise, not only did she not move away, but she rolled over facing me, and pressed her body into mine. We laid there for a minute not uttering a single word but our eyes communicated everything that we wanted to say. We then took turns exploring each other's bodies and touching each other in the places we had only jokingly discussed before. I couldn't believe what was happening and for a moment I thought I was dreaming, but what I was feeling in my body and the way it felt touching hers made everything all too real. I was living out the experience I had read about and I didn't want it to end. We continued that night and for the remaining two nights that we roomed together while out of town. When it was finally time to return home, I figured that we would just leave that experience there and everything would go back to normal, but that wasn't the case. From then on out, whenever we were alone together we were talking about sexual encounters, watching them on TV, or acting them out ourselves. We never put a title or any type of rules or expectations on what we were doing, but it became an unspoken understanding that when we were around one another certain things would happen. She kept a steady boyfriend and in an effort to fit in, I even lost my virginity to a boy that she set me up with. The entire time I was with him I just kept thinking about how different it was and how I preferred the way she touched me and how she made me feel over anything that he was doing. My body had gotten use to how a woman felt and anything else was just strange to me. What started out as a curiosity had spiraled into something totally different! I read a book, watched movies on TV and had some conversations with a friend. Those conversations turned into a weekend experience, and that weekend experience turned into something that took us over three years to shake. That was all the water and oxygen that my little seed needed to start growing.

Chapter 3

I See Growth

So you've put in the work of nurturing the seed, making sure it got all the proper amounts of water and oxygen and getting the temperature just right. Now you start to see something breaking forth through the soil. The tree is finally beginning to grow. It starts off as just a little sprout but at least now you can actually see that there is life there and it's at this point that the real work begins. In order for that sprout to continue growing, it has to be cared for. You have to keep it nourished through watering and make sure that it's exposed to the light. Too much or too little of either one of those things will cause damage to the sprout, but if you can find the right balance you'll ensure that it will spring up just as it was intended. So you get into a routine of caring for your baby tree and before long you notice how well it's growing. Previously, the only people that could see it were those that came into your yard, but now it's gotten to a point where the neighbors are noticing the new life form. It looks a little different from the other sprigs in the yards around you, but it's progressing too fast for you to cut it down and start all over. So you just embrace it for its uniqueness and continue to watch it grow.

I was twenty-three years old and looking to experience a little more of life. Up until this point, most of my time had been spent in church and the only people I had really gotten to know were those I went to church with. However, I was starting a part-time job and thought that would be the perfect opportunity for me to broaden my horizons and my circle of friends. On my first day of training, I met two sisters who were a little older than me, but they seemed pretty down to earth so we started having deeper conversations and getting to know each other. The more I talked to them the more I liked them and the more I felt accepted, but nothing prepared me for the conversation that I walked into one morning. The two sisters were sitting around our production table with a male employee and as I joined them I got a clearer picture of what they were discussing. Everyone in the office knew this particular employee was gay and he was explaining a situation that had taken place between him and another man on a previous date. This opened the door for the sisters to ask certain questions and really get to the juicy parts of the story. As I sat there listening, I couldn't believe that they were having such a graphic conversation in public, but I was already locked in and I was actually hoping that they would continue. They did continue, but I had no idea that their conversation was going to turn its focus to me. "Have you ever been with a girl?" One question . . . Do I answer? Was it even any of their business? If I didn't answer, would they still accept me? It was just one question . . . what harm could it have done? So, I answered. "Yes, I have." One of the sisters gave a smirk and a nod to the other, then, the flood gates opened. That one question led to another question, then another, and another. I felt as if I was being interviewed again but this time it wasn't for employment and with every answer I gave them they got a little more interested in my experiences. This time, I was providing the juicy details that they wanted to hear and they were providing the acceptance that I was longing for. We finished the conversation that morning but our interaction concerning that topic was just beginning.

For the next few weeks I noticed that one of the sisters was paying me quite a bit more attention than the other. We started taking our breaks together, going to lunch together and even passing notes to each other throughout the work day. The notes started out as typical, friendly banter, but it didn't take long for them to take a more sexual turn. Once that turn occurred, we quickly transitioned into more explicit descriptions of things we had done in past experiences and what we wanted to do to each other. It became like a game. What could we say to raise the eyebrow of the other? The more graphic the better, no holds barred. But you can only read someone's sexual advances for so long before you get tired of just reading and you want them to show and prove. So we started making plans of when we could actually see what each other was working with, so to speak. We tried for weeks to set things up but it seemed like everything we planned fell through one way or another, but I was determined. I was tired of playing the PG-13 role with her and other women. I wanted the real deal Holyfield and I wasn't going to let anything stand in my way of getting it. I received a phone call from her one Friday evening and we decided that we were meeting and it was going down that night, no matter what. I got myself together and tried to calm my excitement enough to make the thirty minute drive to where she was. It was like one of those times that you start out heading home and before you know it you're there but don't even remember how you got there because there was so much on your mind. I had so many thoughts running through my head concerning what was about to happen that I didn't realize that I had passed the exit and gone several miles out of the way. My mind had already pressed fast forward and I was so focused on the encounter that I couldn't concentrate on what I was doing. I finally turned around and started driving back towards our rendezvous point. When I pulled into the parking lot, she was there waiting for me and no words even needed to be spoken. She and I both knew exactly what we were there for so we didn't waste one moment on romantic innuendo or gentle caressing. We went inside and barely gave the door time to close behind us before we were kissing and undressing each other. This wasn't like the scene I had read about in that book in eighth grade. It wasn't even like my experiences with my friend when I was a teenager. This time, we could've been starring in one of the movies I had viewed ten years prior on channel 99. She was doing things to me that no one had ever done before and I was completely engulfed in the passion that burned between us. I felt at home. This felt natural. This felt like what I was supposed to have been doing all along. I wasn't afraid. I wasn't questioning. I was going with the flow and everything felt right. I knew it had nothing to do with love or any feelings we had for one another. But physically, it was as if things were finally falling into place for me. It's like a light bulb came on and I could see clearly for the first time in years. Seconds became minutes. Minutes became hours. And those hours became all the evidence I needed that I was where I was supposed to be.

Things ended that night, but our physical relationship was far from over. Every chance we got for the next year, we were stealing away for a hot, intimate encounter and with every encounter I was becoming more and more comfortable with the lifestyle I had chosen. So comfortable in fact, that I decided to talk about it with another friend that I had started spending more time with. I didn't know what her reaction would be, but after she finished telling me about a night that she spent with her boyfriend, she asked if I wanted her to set me up with a friend of his. I saw that as an open door to tell her about the woman from my job that I was sleeping with and how sex with her made me feel. She had so many questions and I was all too eager to answer each and every one of them. We sat on her front porch talking and drinking until the wee hours of the morning, but the next thing I knew, we were kissing. Everything happened so fast that I didn't even know who made the first move or whose idea it was, but there we were. I moved my hand down the front of her body and settled between her legs. As I moved, she moved and there was something empowering about knowing I was bringing her pleasure. Once we finished, neither one of us said a word. I went and got into my car and drove home, but was surprised when I received a text from her asking me to come over again the next night. I wasn't sure what I was going to be in for, but I wasn't about to turn down an invitation. So I went back. When I got there this time, there were more people at the house. We all sat around laughing, joking and of course, drinking. As the crowd started to thin out, I was left on the front porch again talking with my friend and an older friend of hers who was a minister. I was oblivious to anything that this other woman knew about me, but it was apparent that she had heard something because she started asking me questions about my sexuality. I thought it was going to be some kind of religious lesson, but as soon as my friend started giving me accolades on what had happened the night before, I knew it would be a different type of conversation. They both laughed about our little tryst and in my inebriated state, I started to brag about the skills I possessed. I started flirting with the minister friend and I could tell by the way she smiled and giggled that she wasn't as turned off by me as one would have thought. I sat there wondering how far she would let me go, so I tapped into my liquid courage and decided to test the waters and see. I touched her cheek and she didn't

27

pull away. I touched her cheek again and she grinned. At this point, I knew she probably wouldn't stop me from doing what I wanted to do next. So I took a deep breath, leaned in slowly and I gave her a kiss that she was sure to feel in her outermost extremities and her innermost parts. She was so into it that I didn't care one bit that my friend was sitting right beside her. It seemed that my friend didn't mind it, because at one point she took my hand and placed it on her body. There I was, kissing and fondling two different women at the same time, one a friend, the other a minister. I should've been asking myself what was wrong with the picture I was in or how I had gotten myself in that situation, but I was having way too much fun to even think that logically. Although things didn't progress much further than that, I gave both women what they wanted that night and they gave me an ego boost that left me walking a little taller with my head a little higher.

I walked away from that experience feeling different about myself, but more importantly, I had noticed a pattern in how people dealt with me once they found out my secret. In the few years that had passed, there were some friends that learned of my covert lifestyle and things immediately became awkward between us. It didn't take long for them to create distance and I knew that estrangement from them was inevitable. On the other hand, there were friends that I would tell and curiosity would get the best of them and eventually, so would I. This was the routine. This was the tap dance that they all participated in. I let the cat out of the bag and I would either lose a friend or gain a lover.

Coming to this realization, I did what I thought any
person in my position would have done. I used it to
my advantage. From then on out when I met someone
new, I'd give myself time to get to know them and
them time to get to know me. During that getting
acquainted period, there would always come a time
when questions would arise about each other's love
lives and I would use that as my opportunity to test
the waters. In the back of my mind, I knew what I was
doing was wrong, but it had gotten to a point where I
couldn't stop myself anymore. It became automatic.
When I joined a new church, I even told myself that I
wasn't going to be with women intimately anymore,
but unfortunately that declaration didn't last very
long. Within a few months of being there, I met
another older minister and at first, I was amazed by
her gifts and the anointing that rested upon her life. I
observed the manner in which she dealt with others,
prayed for others, and even taught others and I really
began to admire her. It was almost the same feeling
I'd had towards my teacher in seventh grade, but deep
down I knew something about it was different. One
day we were sitting around talking with some other
new members, sharing testimonies and encouraging
one another. The minister started talking about how
the enemy can use things in our past to try and derail
our future. Others added their two cents and then
she mentioned that some people even get tricked
into believing that because of molestation or rape
at a young age, that they are attracted to and better
off with the same sex. When she said this, my ears
perked up like those of a dog that hears a strange
noise at night. I didn't know what in the world would

make her say that and I didn't know why in the world
it resonated so much with me, but I couldn't shake it.
I wasn't satisfied anymore with just being around her
with a group of people. I had to get to know her on a
more personal basis. So I did.

She and I started talking over the phone and spending
some time together outside of church. It didn't take
long for my past to come up and I was intrigued when
she didn't run in the other direction. Even though
my experience with the other female minister was
still somewhat fresh in my mind, I wasn't expecting
the same thing to happen with this one. However,
I couldn't help but wonder why this minister was
remaining in contact with me, instead of cutting me
off like the others that wanted nothing to do with my
lifestyle. The more she allowed me to get to know
her the more my admiration for her grew, but in
addition, the more I realized that our stories were not
all that different. When she first told me about her
experiences with a woman from her past, I couldn't
believe that someone of her spiritual caliber had
actually been with a woman sexually. But the longer
I thought about it, the more I convinced myself that
her reason for telling me about her past was to leave
the door open for me to walk through. So once again I
started testing the waters to see just how open she was
leaving that door.

By now we were spending even more time together
and I used that time to become an expert on
everything concerning her. In my mind, I was just
showing how much I cared about her by learning

what she liked and doing things to make her happy. She committed herself to doing so much for other people, sometimes at her own expense, that it gave me satisfaction to see a smile on her face. That's what I thought was happening. But deep down I was like a thief that spends hours studying the security system of a bank, looking for a weakness and a way in. While on the one hand, I thought I had a found a mentor that I could confide in, learn from, and do special things for, on the other hand, I was just waiting for her to let her guard down so that I could make my move. And after weeks of pushing the limits, the day finally came when she could no longer fight off my advances and she gave in. It was hard to believe what was actually happening, but I was so caught up I didn't care that I was responsible for the fall of my mentor. I didn't care that I was setting her back years. I didn't care that I was jeopardizing the anointing that she carried. I was just doing what I had been doing for years. And I kept doing it. We even began living together only a few months after our relationship became sexual. We both knew that our intimate encounters couldn't continue, but it was like we enjoyed the warmth of the fire and wanted to see just how close we could get to it without getting burned. Well, needless to say, in the two years of our cohabitation, we got burned on more occasions than we could even count. We would go to church together, serve in ministries together, all the while we were fighting against something that was becoming stronger than both of us. I didn't understand why I needed her as much as I did, but even beyond anything immoral, I just couldn't seem to let her go. We went back and forth for the longest. We'd have months where we'd be on the straight and narrow and focused on the path of a strong friendship, but then in a moment of weakness, we would get knocked right back to square one. Eventually, I started noticing that she was doing things to pull away, but in my panic and fear of being abandoned, I said and did things that I knew would pull on her heart strings and bring her back to me. It was selfishness at its best, or should I say its worst. I knew she was just trying to do the right thing, but it felt like she was leaving me in a mess that the both of us created and I didn't know how to handle it. It would've been better if she'd just cut me off in the beginning. At least that way, my emotions would never have gotten so wrapped up in her. The more she pulled away and started building a life without me, the emptier I felt, but I couldn't let her know that. I couldn't be the weak one. I didn't want to be the needy one. So I waited until I knew she would be gone from the house for a long period of time, I packed all of my belongings into my car, and I moved out. I had to leave her before she left me. That's just how it had to be.

The next few months proved to be some of the most difficult of my life. While I tried to put on a brave face and act like I didn't care, I had to endure seeing my former lover with a new boyfriend, dealing with feelings of rejection, and even ostracism from my church. I knew that something had to give, but I had no idea what to do or how I would make it through the situation. I started thinking back on all the things I had been taught about the lifestyle I was living and all the screaming preachers that I'd heard telling people like me to get right. Maybe this was my opportunity to do things differently. Maybe this was God's way of giving me an out. It couldn't hurt to try right?! So I did. I prayed every day and even fasted to the point that I lost twenty pounds. I was begging God to change me, but nothing happened. At that same time, I watched as my church embraced the minister and restored her to her previous positions, but those same people wouldn't touch me with a ten foot pole. I thought the church was supposed to be the place where people got help, but instead it felt like I was getting the cold shoulder. I didn't feel the love of God. I didn't feel the love of my church family. So why would I give up feeling the love of another woman? Why would I give up the only thing that made me feel the least bit secure? The only problem was I continued to choose the wrong women to love. Up until this point, I'd been with women who were just looking for a good time, those who wanted to experiment, or those like this minister, who knew it was wrong, but just couldn't control themselves. This is what needed to change. I wanted to know that a woman loved me for me and that I was the only woman that she would love. Not another lesbian that was used to the touch of a woman. Not another friend that was just curious to see what it would be like to be with a woman. I wanted real love. But how would this even be possible? I remember the moment that I told God what I desired like it was yesterday. I was getting out of the shower one morning and I paused for a second. I looked up and said, "God, I'm tired of being with other lesbians. I want to turn a straight woman." I got dressed and went on about my day, not realizing that my little sprig of a tree had grown out of control.

Chapter 4

How'd This Tree Get So Big?

After all the time you've spent watering your little
tree, making sure it's in the perfect spot to get just the
right amount of sunlight, and caring for it as it grew,
you finally see the fruit of your labor. This massive
life form is now standing multiple stories high in the
middle of your front yard. You got exactly what you
wanted. Once again you ignore the fact that your tree
looks a little off, but it still serves the same purpose
as all the other trees in the neighboring yards. You
can still enjoy the warmth of a nice day in the spring
without the discomfort of sitting directly in the sun.
That same shade cools your home in the summer
time when the temperature outside can be nearly
unbearable. You're able to observe the beauty of the
changing leaves in the fall as the bountiful colors add

more life to the atmosphere. Even as the winter cold rolls in, you look out of your window and smile at the sight of each branch catching the snowflakes as they fall from the sky. And beyond the elegance of what you can see, it's this same tree that provides the oxygen that fuels your life day in and day out. But after a while things start to change. Now, everything that you thought you wanted is causing you more problems than the happiness it once brought. The branches are growing out of control and causing damage to your home. The leaves are cluttering up your yard and its becoming difficult to see any light through the dark shadow that the tree is casting. You had no idea when you started nurturing this tree years ago that it would ever grow to be so big and cause so many problems. But it has. So where do you go from here?

When I stepped out of the shower that one morning and uttered the statement of what I desired to God, I had no idea that only a few short weeks later, I would meet a woman that would change my life drastically. I had just graduated from college and was walking into day one of work on my very first full time job. I was already a ball of nerves just wondering what things would be like and if all the knowledge I'd acquired in school would actually pay off. In addition to that anxiety, I had no clue what type of people I would be working with or what types of relationships, if any, I would form. I entered the room where orientation was being held, found a seat at a table with a group of women who looked somewhat inviting, and began having casual conversations while we waited patiently for things to get started. Then she entered the room. She walked over in her yellow, short-sleeved Tommy Hilfiger sweater and gray slacks, sat down at the corner of the table diagonal from where I was sitting, gave a smile that lit up the entire room, and instantly I was hooked. As everyone at the table talked and got to know each other better, I couldn't put my finger on why I was so drawn to the woman on the other end. After just a twenty minute conversation, I felt like I'd known her for years and anything I didn't know, I wanted to find out. Strangely enough, it wasn't until I sat down to write about this experience that I realized the reason behind the immediate connection. I had met this woman before. I had talked to this woman before. Twelve years prior to this meeting, I was drawn to this woman before. My new colleague was a carbon copy of my seventh grade teacher in looks, personality and spirit. But this time, I wasn't a student looking for a mentor. I was a peer looking for a friend.

So, over the next couple of months we became friends . . . very close friends. The more time we spent around one another, the more things we realized we had in common. It was almost as if we were twins, separated at birth, and by ten years. If having similar personalities, taste and interests wasn't enough, the fact that we were both feminine women who played sports blew our minds even more. Neither one of us had ever met anyone more like us and it was refreshing that we could be ourselves completely and be accepted with one another, a fact which only made us want to spend even more time together. People begin to jokingly say we were joined at the hip, and they were right. Where you saw one, you saw the other. She was my best friend! We talked about everything from our day to day feelings to what types of mothers we thought we'd be. At the time, she and her husband were trying to start a family and she shared her excitement and anxiety about bringing a life into the world. Besides that, she made it a priority to find me a guy so that we could all hang out as couple friends and share our lives together. I'd never had a relationship this close before and I couldn't thank God enough for bringing a person like her into my life. We prayed together, encouraged each other, and had more fun than we'd had with anyone else in our lifetimes. Then one conversation, on our way to play basketball at a local park, ignited a flame that permanently changed our friendship. We were talking about how our lives had been lived in a pretty sheltered manner and somehow we got on the subject of going to night clubs. She stated that she'd never been to one before because it really wasn't her scene. I told her the name of the only club I'd been to and agreed that I wasn't too interested in that type of night life. I chuckled as she spent a minute or two trying to recall if she'd ever heard of the club, before finally admitting that she hadn't. I told her not to worry and that I would've been extremely surprised if she had heard of the club because it was strictly for lesbians. I couldn't help but laugh a little harder when she asked, "Now why would you be going to a lesbian club?" "Because I'm a lesbian," I answered. I sat in the passenger seat of her vehicle and watched as her face changed colors, her forehead wrinkled and her eyebrows rose. I didn't know what was going through her mind but in the awkward moments of silence that followed, I couldn't help but think I had just lost my best friend. When she finally spoke I could tell that her mood and demeanor had changed but she was trying her best not to let it show. I in turn, tried to give reassurance that I wasn't after her in a romantic way but that I would understand if she would be more comfortable with some distance between us. After another couple minutes of awkward silence, she told me that in order for her to continue our friendship she'd have to discuss this new revelation with her husband and make sure he had no objections to us remaining as close as we had become. At that point, I really didn't know what to think, but I resolved in my head that things would never be the same between us. I felt as if I'd lost the best friend I'd ever had simply because I couldn't keep one little detail to myself. The next few days were the longest of my life, waiting to hear what became of her conversation with her husband. If he said to end the friendship, how would that affect our work relationship? How would we explain that to all the people that were calling us "Frick and Frack"? How would I go on without her by my side? There were so many negative thoughts running through my head that when her name appeared on my phone I was afraid to even answer the call. When I finally picked up, I didn't want to make any small talk or waste time asking about each other's day, I just wanted to know if I still had my friend. She must've known that was all I wanted to hear because the first thing she said was "He's okay with it". It was like we both breathed a sigh of relief and the excitement we shared in the remainder of

that conversation was like two kids on Christmas
who had gotten everything they'd asked for. But then
everything in my mind changed and I was faced
with a dilemma that seemed all too familiar. Here
was another woman that knew my secret and didn't
run. What did that mean? Was she curious? How was
I supposed to handle her now? I went from being
excited to keep my friend to wondering what type of
friend she would actually be in the blink of an eye. As
soon as this uncertainty crept in, so did the images of
being with this woman in a manner far more intimate
than anything we had experienced before. I was at the
point of no return, but I had no idea that she would be
willing to go along for the ride.

I got comfortable in the fact that she kept reminding
me she was happily married, so when we joked about
my sexual habits I didn't give it a second thought.
But then the conversations changed and comments
started being thrown around about whether or not I
would be able to satisfy her. That, in itself, confirmed
for me that she was curious and I knew it was just a
matter of time before she gave in to the curiosity. We
had both let down our defenses and opened ourselves
up to something that would eventually overtake us,
but at the time we were just having what we thought
was innocent fun. It didn't take long, however, for
our fun to turn into feelings that neither one of us
could ignore. We stood at an important crossroad,
at which we made the wrong decision. Initially, we
did everything in our power to respect her marriage,
but the more time we spent together after we
acknowledged our feelings for each other, the less

we considered the repercussions to the covenant she was a part of. Then one day after we had finished playing ball, she said something that I never would've expected in a million years. All of our jokes and conversations had come to a head and she decided to make a bet with me that if we were together sexually, I wouldn't be able to make her scream. Being the confident person that I was in that area, there was no way I was going to turn down that bet, but part of me still believed that she was just blowing smoke. So, I called her bluff and to my astonishment, she set a date for when the encounter was to take place. It was only supposed to happen once then we would continue with our friendship the way we had envisioned all along. We were just getting it out of our system so we could get on with our lives . . . or so we thought. We finally experienced that supposed one time, but instead of getting anything out of our system, it solidified our love and tied our souls to the point that we forsook all others to cling to one another. I won the bet that night, but instead of taking the money she had promised, I settled for taking her heart.

From that night on, we were even more inseparable than we were before. Even though our relationship had to remain a secret for various reasons, it was everything that I had ever hoped for and then some. I was in love with this woman and overwhelmed by the fact that she was in love with me. Our affair went on for months and neither one of us had a care in the world. But then she started noticing my increasing disdain whenever anyone mentioned anything to do with her husband. I would sit in the midst of

conversations as people asked her if they were still
trying to start a family and grit my teeth as she
gave general answers regarding their relationship.
I knew the situation when I entered it with both
eyes wide open, but the more my love for her grew,
the less I liked being her dirty little secret. So as a
demonstration of her love for me, she sat me down
one day and told me she willing to end her marriage
if we could have a life together. My initial desire was
to grab her by the hand, walk off into the sunset and
live happily ever after, but the more I thought about it
the guiltier I felt. The crazy thing was, as long as we
were sneaking around I could calm my conscience,
but the thought of causing a marriage to come to an
end was just too much for me to handle. Although I
knew I was committing sin, I felt like there would be
a special place for me in hell if I was responsible for
breaking up a marriage. So I did what I thought was
in both of our best interests and told her that it would
be better if we went back to just being friends. She
seemed to be surprised by my reaction and a little
hurt by it, but we agreed to try and put things back
in order. Unfortunately, that agreement only lasted
as long as neither one of us tried to pull away. If she
drew closer to her husband, I had a problem with
it. If I tried dating someone else, she had a problem
with it. We were in a hopeless game of tug-a-war
that was impossible for either of us to win. I knew I
had to let her go, but I couldn't. I was afraid that she
would replace me in her heart and her bed and my
insecurities wouldn't allow me to do what I knew
was best for her. This was the realest relationship I
had been in and I wasn't willing to lose it. I didn't

realize that by holding onto it so tightly, I was causing damage that would eventually be far beyond repair. But I continued to go against my better judgment and every time she tried to pull away, I would give her the hope that we could build a life together so that she would come back to me.

This game between us went back and forth for a couple of years and all the while, I was ignoring the still, small voice in my spirit that was telling me I was wrong. The closer we got to making plans for our future, the louder that voice became but the more I fought to silence it. I talked to her about what I was feeling and there was a point when she almost had me convinced that I could live my life with her and still live the life that I wanted in God. After all, God is love and He loves everybody, no matter who we happen to fall in love with. She was flourishing in her spiritual walk, so I tried my best to embrace her beliefs, but something within me remained troubled and I couldn't seem to get away from the inner turmoil I was experiencing. It was like there was a battle between my love for her and my love for God and I didn't realize that we were both becoming casualties of that war. I couldn't understand why it was so easy for her to be with me and still call herself a woman of God, but I felt like I had to make a choice between the two. And once again, I made the wrong decision. I put my relationship with God on the back burner so that I could continue playing the game with this woman, a game that eventually turned into a struggle for control.

She could tell that I was unsure about our future but
I kept trying to make her believe that everything was
fine. She was willing to sacrifice so much for me and
just wanted some reassurance that I wasn't going to
leave her out on the ledge by herself. Unfortunately,
there was no reassurance that I could offer, but we
still weren't able to let each other go, and that's when
the distrust settled in. As long as she knew and
approved of my every action she was content and vice
versa, but the trouble came when that knowledge and
approval wasn't there. We started becoming jealous
and suspicious of any person that the other spent
time with, which led us into dangerous territory and
introduced violence into our relationship. She hit me
on two separate occasions when I chose something
else over spending time with her. It taught me that
in order for us to be together, she had to be my first
and only priority. But I wasn't ready for that type of
responsibility and I started fighting for a little control
of my own. At this point, I was angry with myself
that I had chosen this woman over God. I was angry
with God that He wouldn't allow me to be at peace in
this relationship. And I was angry with her because
she had made me fall in love with her and now I
wanted to be free but I couldn't let her go. I felt as if I
had no control over my own life and the only thing I
could control was to get her before she got me. So the
pattern began. Whenever I felt like she was getting
the upper hand I would lash out. I didn't care how
much damage I caused to property or to her because
in those moments, she would conform to my will.
Afterwards, we would go days without speaking,
but we couldn't ignore the magnetic pull that we had

on one another, so the necessary apologies would be made and we would go on as if nothing had happened. We both recognized that this wasn't the relationship that we had hoped for and after a series of trials, tribulations, and police reports, it finally came to an end for what we thought would be the last time.

We lasted for several months without having any contact whatsoever, but then one day she called me out of the blue and asked to meet. I don't think either one of us really knew how to react to the other, so the conversation started out in an awkward manner. We made small talk and inquired on what had been going on in the life of the other but we knew there were weightier matters to be discussed. It didn't take long for the topic of the violence in our relationship to come up and how unacceptable something like that was. I was taking responsibility for my actions and trying to let her know that if we continued in a friendship that things would be different. It seemed at first that she was open to the idea of resuming as friends but the more she talked the less I believed in that possibility. Then she mentioned that she was considering a period of separation from her husband because things weren't working out with them as they had hoped. She was exploring other options and wanted to make the best decision for her and her future. I wondered why she was sharing that information with me, but then she started questioning whether or not we would have made it if things had started out differently. What if she wasn't married when we met? Could I have been happy with her and had a clear conscience if her husband wasn't in the picture? She posed these questions and I couldn't help but ponder them myself. Could we have made it if we didn't have the obstacle of her marriage standing in the way? Sitting across from her at the table that day, I put everything from our past out of my mind and tried to imagine a future with her. This time, I wouldn't be responsible for the breakup of her marriage because they were separating anyway. So, why not give it a shot? Then she specifically asked if I would be able to love her and God at the same time. For the life of me I had no idea if I was capable of doing it, but I had already experienced what it was like not having her in my life and I didn't want to go back to that. So I mustered up an answer that sounded acceptable and we made the decision to give our relationship one more chance. She followed through with the separation from her husband and within a month and half we were moving in together as a couple.

We found a beautiful house that we both loved and moved in with high hopes of having a long and happy life with one another. The first few months were more blissful than I ever could've wished for and it seemed that we were well on our way to a great future. Everything was out in the open now. We were going out on dates, holding hands as we walked in the park and sharing how much we loved each other with everyone around us. Some people accepted our relationship and they became our support system, the ones that didn't, we just brushed off and kept it moving. It was the perfect situation. We had made a home for ourselves and we were finally happy. But just when we began discussing the idea of starting a family of our own, that still, small voice started nagging me once again. I thought I had gotten away free and clear and was actually going to be able to have the life I'd always wanted with the woman that I loved, but it wasn't quite that simple. I was happy, but I had no joy. I was happy, but I had no peace. I was more troubled in the open relationship than I had ever been when we were having the affair. I was living a life that was completely opposite of what I believed God wanted for me, and because of that, I went through mental and spiritual torment on a daily basis. I couldn't even go to sleep at night without being afraid that I wouldn't wake up in the morning and my biggest fear was dying in a life of sin. Needless to say, I lost a lot of sleep, but I still couldn't bring myself to separate from the woman that my soul was tied to. It didn't matter what anyone told me to try and convince me that God still loved me. My truth was that for the first time in my life I couldn't feel His presence and it was complete agony being separated from Him. Once again I was in a situation where I had to choose between my lover and my Lord, but I just couldn't make the decision. I thought that maybe it would be easier if she was the one that left me, that way I wouldn't have to be the one carrying the weight of breaking us up, but the pain of feeling her pull away was nearly unbearable. So what was I supposed to do?

As I remained silent, the distance and tension between us started to grow and all the excitement of our relationship began to fade. It was like we both knew we had come to the end of our journey together, but neither one of us wanted to be the one to say it out

loud. So we didn't. And as she poured herself into
her work, I worked on the only other relationship
that had ever been real to me . . . my relationship
with God. I plugged back into my old church and
began opening myself up again to hear from Him
and figure out His plan for my life. The closer I got
to God, the farther away I was from her, but we still
remained in the same house. When we finally sat
down and had the conversation to end the relationship,
we thought things would get better, but we became
roommates who still shackled each other to the same
expectations and responsibilities of being lovers. It
was an impossible situation. We argued all the time.
The things that we once loved about each other were
now annoying, and it seemed like we couldn't even
stand to be in each other's presence. The only room
we could agree in was the bedroom and in four and a
half years, we had gone from strangers to best friends,
best friends to lovers, lovers to roommates, and
roommates to enemies. It was only a matter of time
before everything came to a head and it finally did as
we resurrected our struggle for control.

When an argument started on a Tuesday morning
that had us both screaming at the top of our lungs, I
knew that it was going to be the straw that broke the
camel's back. She had gotten certain things in her
mind regarding me that were completely false, but
she wouldn't even let me speak long enough to get
the truth out. The more she yelled and talked over
me the more I realized that I lost all control and there
was nothing I could do about it. It was one thing for
us to part ways on good terms, but the thought of her

believing a lie and convincing others of that lie had my emotions in a pressure cooker and I was about explode. There hadn't been any violence between us for months, but unfortunately this argument would change all of that. Her words became like knives piercing into the inner core of who I was and I crossed the line trying to defend my character. I pushed her down on the sofa and the look in her eyes was that of fear and surprise. I had surprised myself and as I held her down I knew that there was no going back for either of us. She pleaded for me to let her up but all I could think in my mind was not to relinquish control back into her hands. What in the world was I doing? This was not me! I didn't know how I had allowed myself to lose all self-control but I was holding both her life and mine in my hands and I had to get it together quickly before anything tragic happened. Without saying another word, I let her up off the sofa, went into the other room and immediately started packing my things. I had to get out of there for her sake and mine and there was nothing that was going to stop me this time. We continued arguing as I stuffed my vehicle with as many of my belongings as I could and when I pulled out of the driveway I knew it would be the last time I would lay eyes on the woman of my dreams. How did we get here? What went wrong? For the life of me I couldn't understand how things had gotten so bad, after all, she was exactly what I wanted. I had asked God for a relationship, for female companionship, and He let me have just what I asked for. I thought it would be the one thing that would bring joy and completion to my life, but instead, it had me near destruction. As I drove around wondering where I was supposed to go from there and how I was supposed to live without her, I realized that I had gotten the one thing I had desired for so long and it was the very last thing that I needed. This tree was too big! I couldn't handle it anymore! And I had to do something about it.

Chapter 5

Chopping Down the Tree

So you're looking around at all the problems that this huge tree is causing to your yard and your home and it seems like there's only one option. Although you still enjoy the comfort and shade that your tree provides, it's gotten to a point where it just doesn't feel the same anymore. Even in the shade you feel exposed and that peaceful feeling that once surrounded you seems to have escaped. Now you begin to wonder if maybe things would be better if you cleared your yard or had a tree like everybody else. It's okay to start over . . . it's just a tree. How hard could it be? So you make the decision to chop it down and try something different. Starting with the branches, you take out the proper tools and start hacking away. It doesn't seem too difficult at first so you think you're on the right track.

One by one the branches fall and you start to feel pretty good about the process. With all the different sizes, some of those branches are harder to cut down than others, but you start to envision the finished product and it motivates you to keep going. Once you've cleared the tree of all its branches, it's time to change out the set of tools you're using and start on the trunk. This takes a little more effort, but you've come too far to stop now. You're determined to get this tree to the ground. You push through the tension, all the flying sawdust, ignoring the burn you feel in your arms until finally, you're able to yell "TIMBER" and watch the massive form fall right before your eyes. You did it! All your hard work has paid off. Mission accomplished . . .

After my relationship ended I knew I had to do something different, but the problem was, my sexual desires didn't change. For almost two decades, I had found solace in the embrace of other women's arms, knowing that it wasn't right, but it was comfortable and enjoyable. So I thought I had come up with the perfect solution. Since it was the relationship that didn't work out, I figured that as long as there was no commitment involved, I would be able to continue sleeping with women without any further issues. So that's what I did. I never set out to meet a woman with the sole purpose of things turning sexual, but whenever I had that certain itch, there seemed to always be a woman there who was more than willing to help me scratch it. During the period of a few months, I met two different women, both married, one of whom was even more experienced in the lifestyle than I was and the other had a growing curiosity but was too afraid to admit it. Both of these women became like fun projects for me, something to play with and pass the time. The one that had the experience was a ball to flirt with, but she was looking for a long-term lover to fulfil the needs that her husband could not. It was exciting to see how far the one who was curious would let me go, but when her friends discovered that she was tiptoeing on the dark side, she started acting brand new. I finally had to face the facts that after what I went through with the last married woman I was with, pushing the limits with either one of these women would be more trouble than it was worth. So I decided to chill out for a while. That was until a different woman started pursuing me and the games began again. She was the friend of a friend and I could tell by the way she reacted when I came around that she was interested in knowing me far beyond a friendship level. I played along because I liked the flirting and the attention but deep down I had no intention of crossing any lines with her. But then alcohol got involved and all the rules of the game were altered. We were at a birthday party where the drinks were flowing and by the end of the night we were both looking a little cross eyed. While sitting at the bar settling our checks, I felt her hand slide to the inner part of my thigh and up to the point where the seams in my pants met. I was way too inebriated to stop her and quite honestly, I really didn't want to. I unbuttoned my pants and sat there inconspicuously as she slipped her hand in between my legs and inside of me. It had been a year since I'd had this type of contact, but my body responded just like it was yesterday. We knew that there wasn't much we could do inside of a crowded restaurant, so we made plans to meet up with each other at a different location once everyone else had gone home. When we got there we started going at it like a couple of horny teenagers but something felt off. We weren't doing anything that I hadn't done countless times before but it didn't feel the same this time. I was going with the flow but for some reason I wasn't getting the same pleasure that I'd gotten in the past. My mind started to wander and my body wasn't too far behind. After a while, it was as if I had left my body and was watching the act on a television screen. Where did the comfort go? It felt more like a routine than anything else . . . just something to do. But why was I even doing it? I didn't love this woman and physically I had completely tapped out. It was then that I realized I didn't want this lifestyle anymore. It hit me like a ton of bricks that somehow my life had gotten off course and I knew I had to chop this tree down and start over.

How hard could it be, right? I didn't know what my future would hold, but I knew it could no longer be held in the arms of another woman. So, I did the only thing that I could think of to do, I started hacking at the outermost branches of the tree. These branches were what everyone could see . . . my behaviors. I knew some of the things I did would be harder to tackle than others and I couldn't take on a task like this on my own, so I turned to God once again and hoped that He would help me along the way. I took the first step a few days after the last encounter I'd had with a female, simply by deciding that it would be the last encounter. I didn't care how comfortable it had been in the past or how much I had enjoyed that type of sexual contact. It wasn't what I wanted anymore. It had caused me entirely too much heartache and I desired more out of life. Would the physical attraction to women miraculously go away? I had no idea. But I did know that if I refused to act on the attraction that it would eventually get to a point where it could be easily managed. I made a conscious decision to walk in a different direction and down went the first branch.

My next challenge was a little more difficult because it made me face my fear of being alone. Up until this point I had surrounded myself with people that were of the same mind as I was, which made it easier to get that certain itch scratched whenever I needed to. My circle of friends consisted of people who encouraged my behavior because it was entertaining to them, friends that were also in that type of lifestyle, and conquests who were all too willing to be conquered again at any time. Clearly there was no way that I would be able to maintain such a drastic change with these people in my corner, so I had to start severing ties. There were some people who I attempted to explain myself to and tell them about wanting to do something different with my life. While a few of them were supportive, others laughed and told me that it would just be a matter of time before I was right back between another woman's legs. I knew then that I was doing myself more of a disservice trying to make people understand and that if I really wanted to be free I wouldn't feel the need to get the support of the ones that connected me to what I was fighting to get free from. So I took to my phone and just started hitting the delete button. I deleted phone numbers, profile pages on social media, email addresses and any other means of contact that I had with these people. After not hearing from me for a while, a couple of them actually tried to reach out and keep in touch, but to my advantage I discovered this wonderful block feature that disallowed any notification of their attempt to contact me. I was cutting myself off from almost everyone around me but it was a necessary step in my transformation process. I did what I had to do and boom, there went another branch.

Then just as I was entering what I thought was the most isolated period of my life, God led me to become a member of a new church and I began getting plugged in with different ministries there. I kept to myself at first, but the more I got involved the more I noticed connections starting to form with several people. The last thing I wanted was to repeat any patterns from my old churches or old relationships, so as people continued to get close to me and I to them, I was extremely cautious of our level of interaction. There were two women in particular that I took to shortly after we met and our friendships began developing in a healthy manner. Whereas in the past, I would've studied these women to find out their weaknesses and vulnerabilities to use against them, this time, I put forth effort to encourage them and build them up. I could see openings with both of them, cracks in their foundations that would have made it easy for me slip in and turn things sexual before they would even know what was happening, but I covered them. Instead of preying on their insecurities, I prayed that God would strengthen them in those areas so that neither I, nor anyone else could take advantage of them. I was protecting my friends, my sisters, and another branch fell to the ground.

Although I could tell that I was making some real progress, work remained to be done none the less. There were still a few things standing in the way of where I wanted to be but I was determined to put in the work to get there. I started paying attention to what I watched on television, the type of music I listened to and the conversations I had, and I noticed that the majority of those things were bathed in sexual undertones. One of my favorite TV shows to watch reruns of was centered on a group of lesbian friends, their daily interactions and complicated love lives. At first, I justified my continual viewing of the program by saying I was just being entertained by the plot and it wasn't actually influencing me in any way, but it was keeping me tied to that lifestyle. When I'd hear music on the radio that made reference to having sex or making love, I would envision myself acting out the words with another woman, whether the song was painting that picture for me or not. Even in the conversations that I participated in, I would find some way to work sex into the mix, which made it virtually impossible for me to keep my thoughts in line. These things had to change and I had to change them. I had to immerse myself in the complete opposite of what I had been subjecting myself to. So for everything on television that put me in a sexual state of mind, I cut it out of my viewing schedule. Every song in my playlist that provoked a certain sensual mood, I replaced with music that expressed my love for God and His love for me. When I spoke to friends I made sure that the conversations were pure in nature and gave no place for old topics to creep in. Before I knew it, I looked around and all the branches were cut off. My behaviors were finally different, but I was still left with this big tree trunk in my yard that had to be dealt with.

So I had to switch my tools and start in on what the behaviors were connected to. I wondered why the desires had gotten so strong and I had to examine how I viewed myself. It started out as a label that someone placed on me, but in all the years that followed, I had embraced being a lesbian and happily referred to myself as such. Logically, in order to change that mindset, I had to do a lot of internal work and it began with renouncing that title. It was imperative that I start speaking of myself and to myself in a different manner, so when I looked in the mirror it became a priority to recite that I was made in the image of God and there were no mistakes in my creation. I had to tell myself that I wasn't a lesbian, that it wasn't the life God had for me and that I could thrive on a different path. I was deprogramming myself from everything I had allowed to be downloaded in my spirit, and as soon as my viewpoint changed, so did the way I carried myself. People began to notice that there was something different about me and I was enjoying the new confidence I was finding in God. It wasn't just that I was talking to Him more, but He was talking to me and I was hearing Him clearly. For the first time, my relationship with God was the most important one to me and getting more acquainted with Him and His love for me gave me the strength that I needed to push through the trunk of that tree and watch as it hit the ground.

That was my final step . . . right? I had chopped down the tree and my work was done . . . or so I thought. Little did I know that my work was just beginning and I had yet to even experience the most difficult parts of my process. I had taken a huge step, but it was months before I realized that just because I chose to refrain from a particular act or lifestyle did not mean that I was free from it. The tree and all its branches were on the ground, but I was still far from being alleviated of the residual effects of its presence.

Chapter 6

Planting New Grass

Alright! Now that the tree is gone, you can finally do what you want to do in the front yard. You start brainstorming and trying to come up with some new landscaping ideas, but you don't want to take on too much, just something simple. You plant a few flowers, add in some stones in a nice little pattern, and things finally start to have a different feel, but you want more. How about some new grass? You take measurements of the front yard and get all the items and tools you need to begin planting that grass, but there's one thing that you failed to consider. Although the tree is in fact gone, you left the stump in the same place. All the measurements you took now have to be recalculated to account for this tree stump in the middle of the yard. People tell you that you can just plant around it and you try to do that in hopes that maybe, just maybe it'll blend in. But it doesn't. You can visualize the type of landscaping that you want but this stump is sticking out like a sore thumb. You thought you were done with this old tree, but no matter what you try to do in the yard, the stump keeps getting in the way. You try to ignore it because people are bragging on the beauty of the new things that you're doing, but you know that you can't, in good conscience, leave your yard in this condition. By now, there's even a bud growing out of the top of the stump and you're at your wit's end as to what to do next. You put forth so much effort to cut down that tree and you hate to see the process end like this. There has to be a better solution. But what is it?

These were my thoughts as I cleared out the debris from my former lifestyle. I was excited to see what else God had in store for me and I was trusting Him to lead me in the right direction. For the first time in my life, I was building new, healthy relationships and learning exactly what it meant to be a true friend, to have true friends, and even have friends close enough to me that they became family. My world was completely different and I was enjoying every aspect of it. Then all of a sudden, like I had stepped out from behind a curtain, men started noticing me and showing interest in ways that I had never realized before. It was almost comical the number of guys that were flocking to me, for lack of a better phrase, after I made the decision to turn away from women, but each one that approached got the same speech from me. I was very clear that I didn't want to be in a relationship and was only looking to make new friends and find some cool people to hang out and do things with.

I also made it clear that there would be no sexual benefits to my new friendships and it was even more comical at the number of those men who subsequently disappeared. But then I met another gentleman that seemed to be a little different from the others. In the first real conversation we had, I gave him the same disclaimers I had given to other men and when he told me that he was seeing someone, I figured he would be a safe person to begin a friendship with. We would talk about our goals in life, the different sports we played and were interested in, and our relationship with God. It was refreshing to be able to have conversations with someone else without all the pressure of trying to impress them or wondering what they thought about me. It was casual and comfortable and I liked it. But then our conversations began getting longer and longer. He would call me first thing in the morning, last thing at night, and wanted to talk for hours throughout the day. It got to a point where I began to wonder when he ever talked to his girlfriend if he was spending all this time on the phone with me, but when I asked him about her, the only explanation he offered was that she lived in another state. I really didn't think anything else of it until he started leading our talks in a different direction. He knew of my past relationship and my history with women, but I still wasn't sure what to think when he started asking me if I was ready for "this". What "this" was he referring to? I mean I was open to the possibility of settling down with a man, but I knew I was in no position to do it at that point, so I just kept giving him the same answer. "I'm ready when it's in God's timing." But then one night he called and said he had to share something with me, so I met him at one of the places that we'd go to hang out. When I got out of the car he told me that he was free, pulled me close to him and gave me a kiss. Um . . . first of all, I was wondering when in the world he got it in his mind that it was okay to kiss me, and secondly, what was he free from. He told me that he was officially single and asked if he and I could give a deeper relationship a try. In a matter of a few seconds, I think over a hundred thoughts scampered through my head. I was a little nervous about giving him any type of answer, but I could recall all the times I'd heard someone say that the best relationships were built on friendship, so I figured that it wouldn't hurt for this new friend of mine to be my introduction to dating men.

So we started dating and things were fun and exciting at first. It made me smile when he did nice things for me and I enjoyed doing things that I knew he would appreciate as well. But then, out of the blue, it was like someone pressed the fast forward button and everything between us started to speed up. With the expectations that were being placed on me, I felt like I had gone from friend to wife-in-training in a matter of a few days. The fun and excitement didn't exist anymore and I started to feel as if he was trying to turn me into his little woman. He stopped asking if I was free to hang out and do certain things and just assumed that my leisure time would be spent with him. He was crowding my space and even trying to lead me spiritually in a direction that I didn't feel like God was wanting me to go. Now I had experienced women with dominant personalities in the past, but this was on an entirely different level. I saw so many red flags, but everyone around us talked about what a cute couple we were, so I swallowed what I thought was my pride and just rolled with it. This was what it meant to be submissive. From everything I had been taught, the man was supposed to make the decisions and the woman was supposed to submit, as the Bible said, and follow his leading. But something just felt wrong. I thought the problem was that I had gotten used to being in relationship with women and that it would just take me some time to get used to men in this way, but things didn't get any better. I was a fish out of water, but I put a smile on my face and suffered in silence because I wanted to make a change and I thought this was the right thing to do. At this point, no one in my circle of friends knew of my former lifestyle, so it was difficult trying to make them understand why I wasn't all giddy about the relationship. When I finally opened up and shared some of the details of my past, a few of them applauded me for making the change as if it were as easy as flipping a switch. But it wasn't that easy. On top of the general fears I had about the relationship just based on the red flags I was noticing, I had never had a pleasurable, sexual experience with a man and I couldn't imagine that things would be any different with this man if we ever tied the knot. I wish I'd had a dollar for every time someone told me, "Things will be different when you're with someone you love and the sex is in the confines of marriage," because then I could retire to my own private island without a care in the world. But hearing them say this didn't make it any easier. I was terrified, but once again I thought it was what I was supposed to do, so I continued to roll with it. Everyone was so happy for us but they had no idea of the struggle that I was dealing with on a daily basis. It wasn't until my best friend asked me if I was truly okay with the magnitude of my life's changes that I really stopped to question if this relationship was in my best interest. I knew my answer to that question, but I didn't know what to do with it.

I had to admit to myself that I wasn't okay. But it was more than just the differences in our personalities that was causing me to pump the brakes. It was more than my fear of not enjoying sexual intimacy with a man that made me want to shut down. I was afraid of turning back. I could actually peak into my future and see myself with a husband, a child or two, and a female lover on the side, but I didn't want that type of life. I wanted to be a faithful wife and build a good, Christian home for my children to grow up in, but I couldn't shake the thought that my past would come back to bite me. I knew I had to talk to him about what I was feeling and I finally built up enough nerve to have the conversation. I don't know what response I was expecting, but when I asked for a little time and space to make sure that my former life was completely dead, I was confident that he would be supportive. I was wrong. His words echoed support, but his actions were the complete opposite. Instead of giving me space, he became even clingier. Instead of slowing down and giving me time, he continued talks about marriage and our future life together. I felt like I was smothering but I thought I could handle it, until my old desires started to resurface. In the uncomfortable situation that I found myself in, my mind went back to the last time I felt comfort, and that was with a woman. I tried to fight the images in my head and the urges in my flesh but they kept growing with each passing day. The more time I spent with this gentleman, the more I wanted to return to my old way of living. The more he told me he loved me, the more I wanted to hear those words from a woman. He would reach out to hold my hand and I would flinch. He tried to hug me and my whole body would tense up. I didn't understand what was going on or why I was having such a strong, negative reaction. This was what I was supposed to do, right? This was the type of relationship that I was supposed to be in, right? So why was it that the closer I got to him, the more I wanted to sleep with a woman? I thought I was doing the right thing, but this stump kept getting in the way. I even noticed that my feelings for the two women closest to me, those that I mentioned in the last chapter, were beginning to change and I was desiring far more than a sisterhood with them. It got to a point where I was seeing the openings again, but instead of covering them, I started imagining what it would be like to take advantage of any opportunity to have sex with them. I didn't want to jeopardize the friendships I had formed, so when my frustration had grown to a level that I couldn't hide anymore, I had no other choice but to end the relationship and I found myself back in the place where I'd vowed never to return.

I started spiraling out of control and doing things that I never thought I would do. Like a drug addict on the verge of going through withdrawals, I was searching everywhere for a sexual fix to calm the urges I was feeling. To keep from having to go through the whole getting to know you stage, I figured it would be easier just to meet someone online, who would know up front the purpose of our interaction. So I joined a lesbian dating site and specified that I was only interested in discrete, intimate encounters. My profile was a big hit and within a day I had numerous women interested in hooking up whenever I was ready to take that step. Even though I wanted to scratch the itch again, something deep down kept stopping me from actually going through with any plans I made with the women from that site. But then my ex lover's birthday rolled around and the storm started to brew. It was a day that I had been dreading for some time, but I had no idea the immense affect it would have on me. My emotions were all over the place and I couldn't shake the feelings of missing her, hating her, and everything in between. If that wasn't enough, on that same day I found out that the man I had just broken up with, the man that was pushing me into marriage, was now soothing his loneliness by turning his attention to someone I knew. On any other day it wouldn't have hit me as hard as it did, but on this particular day, it was the straw that broke the camel's back.

It was a Friday evening and all I wanted was someone to wrap their arms around me and tell me everything was going to be okay. But instead of finding the solace that I needed in God or a friend, I turned to a bottle . . . a couple of bottles to be exact. I got so drunk that night that I could barely stand, but the bigger problem was, I didn't want to stay at home alone, so I decided to venture out. My inhibitions were down, my judgment was off and I was on a crash course for disaster. I had determined in my mind that I was going to sleep with somebody that night, but it was just a matter of figuring out who. So, I started with one of the women who I previously mentioned. I had never approached her inappropriately before, but I decided to share how deeply my love ran for her and test the waters to see if it was a night that her guard was down and maybe I could slide into one of those cracks in her foundation. I sent her a text message saying exactly what I wanted to do to her sexually and waited to see if she would nibble on the bait. I knew that if she responded in any way it would be a sign that she was possibly open to fulfilling my fantasy. I didn't want to be with some random chick, but as my impatience grew while waiting on that sign, I chose to move on to the next option on my list, the dating site. There was one woman in particular, who was all too willing to meet up with me, and although I had avoided contacting her prior to this day, I reasonably deduced that if I reached out, she would definitely reach back. And she did. I met up with her that night, went back to her place and spent hours fulfilling every sexual desire that I had. But this time it didn't even feel like a routine . . . it felt wrong. I knew I was wrong, I knew I was putting my life and safety in danger and I knew I was going back on a promise I'd made to myself and to God. When I finally made it back to my vehicle I wanted to drive it off a cliff, but I ended up at the home of the other woman who I previously mentioned. I didn't even want her to look at me because of the guilt and shame that I felt and I knew on top of everything else, I had let her down as well. I laid in my friend's arms and cried and she held me until I calmed down, but if she had known what was going to happen next, she probably wouldn't have let me in her house. As soon as my emotional breakdown subsided, the desires rekindled and I started trying to touch her in ways that I knew I shouldn't. My mind was screaming at me to stop, but I needed to feel something other than what I was feeling at that time. I kept pushing the limits, but to my surprise she never pushed me away. She refused each advance that I made, but she wouldn't let me go. The rejection that I felt in those moments was tremendous, but the love that she was expressing to me was far greater. Somehow she had found the strength to do what I'd been hearing from church people for years . . . hate the sin, but love the sinner. It was then that I went from being embraced by a friend to feeling like I was wrapped in the arms of God. I'd never felt a love like that before but I knew it was a love that I couldn't live without. With everything within me I wanted to stay right there and not break the connection, but I had to leave to ensure that I wouldn't do anything else to overstep boundaries. I got in my vehicle and started heading home but the feelings of guilt, shame and confusion began to overtake me and I had to get help.

It just so happened that my church was having a prayer service that night and I fought with every fiber of my being to get there. I told God that I needed a specific touch from Him that night or else I couldn't promise that I would be around much longer. I walked into the sanctuary after the service had already started and I stood behind everyone else with a hat pulled down over my eyes and my head down. I didn't want anyone to see me but God, but I was so burdened with what I had done that I was in a situation once again where I couldn't feel His presence. The service ended and I walked out disappointed that I was still carrying the same load and afraid of what I might do to free myself of it. I got all the way to the door and my cell phone started vibrating in my pocket. It was the assistant pastor of the church saying that our pastor wanted me to come back into the sanctuary. When I walked back in and saw the woman who I had sent the text message to standing up front, I figured I was being called back to receive some sort of rebuke or possibly even put out of the church. But on the contrary, my pastors cleared the room and began to pray for me. They began to call out every single emotion I was feeling and every struggle I was dealing with and all I could do was cry. God was showing his love for me and how much He cared about me through my leaders and there wasn't a doubt in my mind about it. He had heard me when I cried out to Him and this was His answer back to me. In those moments God began to tell me what my next steps needed to be. In order to get rid of the stump that kept getting in my way, I had to put in a bit more work. It wasn't enough just to stop the behaviors and what they were connected to, I had to get to the root of the issue. The stump was still a hindrance because it was still being fed by its root system. There was still life there. In order for me to truly be free, I had to dig a little deeper, find the root and with God's help, pluck it up. This was when my story changed. And this was when the work got real!

Chapter 7

Getting to the Root

The part of tree growth that cannot be predicted is when the seed actually takes root. No one sees it happen or knows exactly how long it will take, but the tree has to grow down before it can ever grow up. It's the root that breaks through the hard shell of the seed and leads to what we see above ground, so in order for you to properly dig up the root system of a tree, you first need to know what type of root you're dealing with. How does it grow? Is it the type that spans out parallel to the ground or does it extend straight down beneath the tree? To gain full understanding, you have to study the tree, identify what kind it is and look at all of its stages of growth. If you know you have an oak tree in your yard, you can find information on the patterns of its root and then decide the best course of action for the uprooting process.

When I made the decision to choose a different path for my life, I thought I was dealing accordingly with the issue of lesbianism. Unfortunately, it took me a while to realize that I was only dealing with one issue and not looking at the complete identity of my tree. Sleeping with women wasn't my only problem. I had taken on a victimizing mentality, analyzing women for weaknesses and insecurities that I could prey on. Somehow, I had learned to control and manipulate other people to get the things that I wanted and I had to figure out when and how these qualities had taken root in my life. It wasn't until I was sitting and listening to the conversation that two other women were having about their pasts that God shined a light on the darkest part of my history, a period of two years that I had completely blocked out.

I was a twenty year college student looking for a place to belong, but didn't know much outside of church and school. I had experimented with some things as a teenager, as you previously read, but I was at a point where I was trying to live on the straight and narrow, so if life didn't happen in one of those two places, I missed out on it. Then during a summer revival, I went to visit a church with some friends and was immediately drawn to the music, dancing, and exciting atmosphere of the house. It seemed like a fun place to be where I might easily fit in, so I started attending on a regular basis. I thought I would be able to go to this church, make some new friends and learn more about God, but little did I know that a woman in leadership there would teach me everything I needed to know about becoming a predator.

The church was small and centered on the female pastor, her four daughters, and a few other families that had chosen to plug in. It didn't take long for me to begin making friends with the daughters that were around my age and I was ecstatic when they started inviting me over to their home to hang out after church and on days during the week. I was getting along with everybody, but the more I came around, the more I noticed that one of the older daughters never really paid me too much attention. I didn't get offended, but instead just attributed that to her being a prophetess and not wanting to get too acquainted with me in a social manner. I respected her, her office and the anointing that she carried, but it only took one night to change all of that. I was spending the night at the house one Saturday and preparing for church the next morning, but I was restless and couldn't go to sleep. I thought everyone else had turned in for the night, but she was still awake and we sat and talked for the first time. The conversation began in a pretty normal manner. She asked how I was enjoying the church and talked about what a valuable asset I had become, but then she surprised me and took things to a much more personal level. All of a sudden she started telling me about this guy she was interested in and asking me questions about my love life. I really didn't even have a love life and it had been over three years since my last encounter with my teenaged friend, so I had no idea what to tell her. I hesitated for a minute because I wasn't sure how she would react if I told her the truth about my past, but when she kept pressing me for answers I finally spilled the beans. She didn't have the reaction that I thought she was going to have, but instead just asked me a few more questions about those experiences then said she would pray for God to give me clarity on what I needed to understand and for Him to rid me of that curiosity. I thanked her for her prayers and support and we went on talking about something else, so I thought that was the end of it. But after another hour or so, the topic of sex resurfaced. This time however, she wasn't just asking me about my experiences, she wanted details about what I liked to do and have done to me. Why was she asking me these questions? For the life of me I couldn't figure out what good this information was to her, but I was just so happy she was interested in talking to me, that even though I didn't have all that much to share, I answered every question she threw my way. Up until this point, the only things that I had experienced which I enjoyed were the feeling of a woman's hand between my legs and the caressing of my belly button, which I told her drove me wild. I should've known something was up when she never offered any information about herself, but I was oblivious to her tactics and mode of operation.

By this time, we had reached the wee hours of the morning and it didn't seem like either one of us was getting sleepy. She had been on the computer during our conversation, but decided to go watch a movie in her bedroom and she asked me if I wanted to join her. I unassumingly accepted the invitation, climbed onto one side of her bed and laid next to her as she tried to find something for us to watch. She settled on a particular channel, but after about half an hour I thought she had fallen asleep because I felt her hand graze my side and come to a resting place on my stomach. Surely she had to be asleep. But then one of the fingers on that same hand began to trace circles around my belly button and I knew that something else was going on. I didn't find her attractive, but the way she was touching me in the very spot that I told her was my weakness, was turning me on. She slid her hand inside my shorts, then used the other to grab my right hand and placed it inside of hers. My mind was blown by what was happening but I was a little too aroused to stop it. I gave her exactly what she wanted and after she reached her climax she told me I'd better go back out to the sofa bed so no one would see me leaving her room in the morning. I think I was still in a state of shock but I knew the best thing was for me to get out of that room. So I went back out into the loft area where I was supposed to be, but there was no way I could actually go to sleep after that. The only thing I could do was lay there and wonder what was going to happen in the light of day. How was I going to face her? How would we ever stand in the same church come morning? My goodness! Would our pastor be able to sense what we did and call us out? I had no idea what was going to happen but I didn't even want to go to church.

As I laid there wondering and fretting, hours crept by and morning finally came. The daughter came out of her room and began getting ready for church as if nothing had occurred. Our paths crossed a few times but neither one of us spoke a word about what we had done only a few hours prior. Once we got to church, everything went on as usual but I felt like I had a two

ton weight bearing down on my shoulders. I couldn't
lift my hands, I couldn't even lift my head for that
matter because of the guilt and shame that I felt. I
didn't want to draw any undue attention to myself
but I just couldn't go through the motions knowing
that I had done something that I shouldn't have. I
was standing there with my eyes closed, repenting
and asking for God's forgiveness and I felt someone's
hand touch my forehead. Someone was praying for
me. I couldn't make out the voice at first but then they
leaned in and I knew exactly who it was. It was her.
The same voice that I'd heard telling me how to touch
her and moaning in ecstasy was now praying for my
complete deliverance and freedom from sin. Really?
I couldn't believe that she was actually praying for
me. I thought for sure that God was about to send a
lightning bolt straight through the roof of the church
to strike both of us dead, but nothing happened.
She finished with me and went on to pray for and
prophesy to several other people in the church and I
just stood there waiting for somebody to sit her down.
I didn't understand why they were letting her operate
so freely or how she even had the audacity to step
into the pulpit after laying with me the night before.
Something was off but I was in no position to say
anything about it, so I kept my head down, my mouth
shut and just prayed to myself as things continued. I
went home that day questioning so many things, one
of which was my further attendance at that church,
but I didn't know where else I would fit in and really
didn't want to start over. I figured I would just focus
on whatever it was God had for me to learn and
put everything else out of my mind. I wouldn't pay

attention to the wrong doings that I saw because it was God's job to judge, not mine. So I went on about my business.

The following weekend, I was back at the house and once again she and I ended up alone in the same room after everyone else had turned in for the night. This time, however, she wasn't all that interested in talking out in the open, but said she wanted to show me something in her room. In my head I was totally skeptical of anything she did or said, but I gave her the benefit of the doubt and thought that maybe this would lead to an apology, or an explanation, or something. So I went into her room and sat on the side of her bed while she placed a video tape in the VCR. She turned off the light and laid down on the other side of the bed, then the movie started to play. It was a porno flick. I wanted to get up and run out of the room but before I could move she tapped me on my knee, spread her legs wide and told me to "Come on". I couldn't believe I had gotten myself in this situation again but I didn't know what she would do or say if I refused, so I put my hand between her legs and gave her what she wanted. Just like the last time, when she was done she told me to leave the room and the next day acted as if nothing out of the ordinary had taken place. We went to church just like normal, but this time, instead of praying for me she started rebuking me openly for allowing sin and shame to control my life. *What*? Now I was really confused. But, she was the prophet so I had to respect who she was and what she was saying. So, I endured the berating even though my spirit was crushed and I left feeling

worse than I did when I'd come in. When I received
a text from her later that day I wasn't sure that I even
wanted to open it. What else did she have to say to
me? Whatever it was I really didn't want to hear it, but
I read the message anyway. She told me that no matter
what happened, I had to stop letting myself get down
and showing the world that I was defeated. She went
on to say that God knew our hearts and He knew and
understood what desires we had, so we shouldn't let
the times that we slip stop us from praising Him. It
didn't seem like there was too much validity to what
she was saying, but again, she was the prophet, so I
took her words as law and resolved within myself that
I needed to do better.

The next time we were together didn't go quite the
same as other times because she had something
different in mind. This time, she told me to come
take a ride with her to the store. I felt pretty safe
with that because there wasn't too much that could
happen out in public. We pulled up in the parking lot
of a movie rental store and she told me to go in and
get a very specific type of movie. She wanted me
to rent something that exclusively showed scenes of
oral sex being performed on women and told me to
make sure I got the right one. I went into the store and
embarrassingly looked around in the porno section
trying to find something she would like. I finally
stumbled upon a video that specified it was all oral
and there were two women on the front cover and
still shots of scenes with other women on the back.
I knew she wanted to see this particular sexual act,
but I didn't know if she wanted to watch two women

doing it. I tried finding another video but I couldn't tell from the titles or pictures what the entire movie would focus on, so I took a chance and checked out the other one I had found. I kept my head down the entire time I was at the counter because I didn't want the video clerk to get a good look at me renting this movie. When I finally got back to the car I gave her the bag with the video in it and didn't say a word as she reviewed my choice. Out of the corner of my eye I could see her nod her head and put the tape back in the bag. Then she pulled out of the parking lot and drove us back to the house. By this time I kind of knew that she wanted something that night, so when we got back and everyone was already asleep, I wasn't shocked when she told me to go to her room and put the tape in. Once again I sat on the side of the bed while she turned out the lights and laid down beside me, but this time, she didn't tap me on my knee. Instead, she undressed from the waist down, grabbed my arm and pulled me on top of her. She pushed down on my shoulders until my body was aligned how she wanted it, then proceeded to coach me through how to perform oral sex on her. I was so nervous because I had never done this before or had it done to me, but she wanted what she wanted and I knew I had to give it to her. Once the instructions ceased, I could tell she was enjoying it by the noises she made and the way her body moved, but I just wanted her to hurry up and climax so I could stop. To say that I was uncomfortable would've been an understatement, but for some reason I couldn't muster up the gall to tell her no and she knew it. From that night on, whenever she would give me a certain look, it was my cue that she wanted me to perform, and every time she gave me that look, I gave her what she wanted. It became a routine. There was no sweet talk, no cuddling afterwards, or anything else that would suggest she cared about me in any way. She was the puppet master and I was attached to the strings.

This went on for months and all the while I had to watch her minster from the pulpit, many times the morning after she made me perform in her bed. It became common that on those mornings I would have to endure severe rebukes from her, but I got used to the song and dance, so I stopped letting it get to me. I reached a point where I acted the same as she did, like there wasn't anything going on. I would walk into a church service and feel absolutely nothing. No guilt, no shame, but no anointing either. I had become numb. I had learned how to put on a show but the presence of God was nowhere in it. I had also learned to enjoy the things she made me do and even began to crave them when I wasn't with her. This woman had taken complete control over me and I could no longer even see the need to get free. I was so entangled that when I received the invitation to move in with the family I happily accepted. I saw nothing wrong with living under my pastor's roof and performing oral sex on her daughter just a few feet down the hall from where she slept. This became my norm. But then one night something happened that shook me to my core and made me realize that I had to run for my life. I was lying in bed about to go to sleep but received a text message from this woman telling me to come into the adjoining room. When I walked in she was underneath the covers, but pulled them back to reveal her naked lower body, legs wide open, and then motioned for me to come to her. Without saying a word, I walked over to where she was, placed my head between her legs and did what I knew to do. She climaxed just like always, but this time when I got up to walk out of the room she stopped me and told me to come and sit beside her on the bed. I was a little confused and definitely didn't know what was coming next but I did what she told me to do and sat down. She then proceeded to tell me how proud she was of how far I had come in God and since she knew she could trust me there was one more thing she wanted me to do for her. She got up and went into the closet for a second and when she came out she was holding a rubber penis in her hand. I had never seen a dildo before and had no idea what she wanted me to do with it, but she climbed back in bed, put it in my hand, then guided my hand between her legs. How was it that one minute she was talking about my progress in God and now she was making me put a sex toy inside of her? This was wrong on so many levels, but I still didn't have the courage to say no. I laid there and thrust this object into her as she spoke out obscenities, but the whole time I was crying and silently asking God to give me the strength to get free. When she finished, she told me I could go back to my room and I walked away determined that she would not control another moment of my life. I knew this was not something that God was pleased with and I had to do something or my soul was in jeopardy of eternal damnation. I didn't sleep at all that night because I was packing my things. I had made up my mind that

I was leaving and never looking back. When morning came, I waited for everyone to leave the house, then I packed up my car and drove away. As the house became smaller and smaller in my rear view mirror, I felt a sense of relief, but I knew that I still had some unfinished business regarding the church.

As I drove around trying to figure out where to go, I called a friend of mine, who just happened to be another older daughter of my pastor, and told her about what had been going on between her sister and me. I wasn't telling her in an effort to expose her sister or make her sister look bad. I was telling her because I wanted to be free from what had entangled me and I needed help to do it. I didn't know what her reaction would be, but after the initial shock and lecture she gave me about wrongdoing, it was refreshing that she offered me her support in confronting the issue and getting passed it. I wish I could say that everyone in the family was just as supportive, but I wasn't that lucky. When the information was revealed to my pastor, her reaction was quite the opposite. She called a meeting at which she was going to present me with a letter she had prepared, banning me from the church. I arrived at this meeting and the entire church was there. She told her daughter to stand and address the congregation and the daughter proceeded to tell everyone how I was spreading lies about her and all she had ever tried to do was pray for me and lead me in the right direction. She went on to say it was clear that the demons that possessed me were out to get her and she had to do whatever was in her power to protect herself and let God deal with me. I sat there

as calmly as I could as she spoke those words and
just prayed that I wouldn't end up in jail for inciting
a riot at a church. After the daughter sat down, the
pastor told me to stand and answer for the lies I had
been telling about the sexual nature of my relationship
with the prophet of the house. I stood up, but before
I could say a word, the pastor instructed three other
women to surround me and she stood in front of me
pressing a Bible to my chest. I opened my mouth and
started talking, but she began speaking in a tongue as
the other women walked in circles around me doing
the same. The louder I talked, the louder they got
and my frustration was getting to a level where I was
about to explode. Finally, as loud as I possibly could,
I screamed out that her daughter had been making
me eat her out for over a year and a half. As soon as
I said this, the pastor spit in my face and I must have
blacked out, because the next thing I remember I was
being held down by two men and a woman with my
arms and face full of scratches and my clothes ripped
to shreds. I looked across the room and the daughter
was on the floor in one corner and the pastor on the
floor in another. To this day I still don't know what
happened in the time that I lost, but it was enough to
seal my fate at that church. When the pastor stood up
again, she told me that I wasn't welcomed and that
I needed to take my lying and homosexual demons
somewhere else. I watched as the daughter smirked
in the corner then got up and thanked her mother for
believing her and ridding the church of this evil. My
body was hurting from the ordeal, but my spirit was
utterly destroyed. I never thought I would've been
in a situation like this in a church and in my heart I

knew I could never let it happen again. I vowed that
I would never allow anyone else to gain that much
influence on me, and I walked away with a totally
different outlook on people and church leadership.
The only problem was I didn't realize that this woman
had already caused more damage than I thought. Her
example had trained me a little too well and in my
effort to not be in the position I was in ever again, I
became her. I left her that day, but she didn't leave me.
It wasn't until over a decade later that I realized I was
carrying her spirit. I was her little disciple, mimicking
my master. Her actions became the root of my issues,
but now it was my responsibility to dig them up.

Chapter 8

Digging up the Root

Now that you know what type of root you're
dealing with, you can start on the task of digging
it up properly. There are some simple steps that, if
followed, will make the process more manageable and
will ensure that you can permanently eliminate the
tree stump, its root system and all the problems that
it may cause. You start by digging a trench around
the stump, a few feet away from the base. The further
away from the stump you are the better, because that
allows you to get to the smaller roots which will be
easier to cut. As you dig, you push the soil outward so
that you can expose as many roots as possible. Once
the trench is made and you can see the roots, it's time
to switch to a sharper tool and start cutting around
the perimeter of the stump. For the best results, you
go around the stump several times using the tool to
stick into the soil and open up the trench by moving

the tool back and forth slightly. Each time you do this it severs the attached roots and begins to loosen the stump from underneath. You don't see immediate results, but you know that as long as you continue with this process, the stump will begin to move. Before long, all the roots are cut and you're then able to pull the stump out of the ground with ease. Now, your work to get rid of this tree is finally done. No more branches. No more stump. No more roots connecting anything to your front yard. The space is free and clear!

So after years of dealing with all the external issues, I realized what type of root my tree was attached to and it was time for me to dig it up. I started with counseling and thankfully, I was able to find a therapist who was a much stronger Christian than I was. She encouraged me to pray and ask God for direction for our counseling sessions and even took the time to pray for me during our appointments. I began talking about the things that had happened to me and what I'd done to other people, and with her help, I started digging the trench to expose the root system. This gave me a chance to bring certain things out in a safe environment without the fear of being judged in any manner and she was able to give me a very balanced view of both the spiritual and natural side. She didn't beat me down with the Bible, but was always able to offer Biblical principles and insight that applied to everything that came up. The more we talked, the more I was able to uncover, even when I wasn't in her presence, so I kept on digging. For the first time I was able to talk about being manipulated and being manipulative, being a victim and becoming a victimizer, transforming from someone who was afraid of sex into someone who used it as a coping mechanism and form of control. She started asking me questions about how I felt when different people treated me in certain ways and did certain things. As I sat there and explored how hurt I was and how the feelings had negative effects on my self-image, she would then ask me how I thought others felt when I did some of those same things to them. It was a rude awakening, but something that I had to confront in order move forward, so I kept on digging. I was getting everything out in the open and forcing myself to deal with other people's actions as well as my own, and this time my readiness for change made all the difference. I didn't want to hide anything anymore. I wanted to get free and stay free, so I didn't stop until every last root was exposed.

Then came the time for me to start the cutting process and I had to switch tools. I knew I wouldn't be able to sever each root in my own strength, so I tapped into a little of God's and started using His Word as a two-edged sword. When I began my day, I was reading the Word. When I ended my day, I was reading the Word. And any time throughout the day, if I felt a thought arise that would make me want to turn back, I would read the Word. But I wasn't just reading random scripture passages and hoping that I'd get something out of them. I began studying the very nature of Jesus Christ when He walked the earth, as described in the four Gospels of the New Testament (Matthew, Mark, Luke and John). I wanted to see how He reacted in

certain situations that put undue pressure on Him.
I wanted to know how He handled people that
mistreated Him. I wanted to gain a full understanding
of His personality, so I could try my best to be just
like Him. I continued reading and came across 2
Corinthians 5:17, which said that if anyone is in
Christ, they are a new creation, old things have passed
away and all things have become new, and it cut away
a root that was tying me to my past. Then I went on
to read Romans 8:1 and was reminded that there is
no condemnation to those who are in Christ, and who
don't walk according to the flesh but according to the
Spirit, and I was able to sever another root. As I dug
into the Word, it began to dig into me and I could
see the stump start to wiggle, so I kept on digging.
I looked in 2 Samuel chapters 11 and 12 at someone
like David. Here was a man who sinned greatly, but
was still said to have the heart of God and went on
to write the majority of the Psalms recorded. He was
able to be used mightily once he acknowledged and
turned away from his sin. I also noticed how Paul,
originally named Saul, was a persecutor of the church
in Acts 9, but through the transformation power
of God, was able to reach countless souls for the
kingdom. Everything that I read was providing me
with further evidence that God wouldn't hold anyone
to their past sins, mistakes and failures if they were
willing to face them and do something different. The
process was working and I was seeing even more
movement in the stump. Things stopped affecting me
in the same way they had before. I stopped having
the same destructive reactions to life's stressors and
started loving myself and seeing myself as God loved

and saw me. I was a new creation. I had cut away
as many of the roots as I could see but one thing
remained that was preventing me from pulling up the
stump completely.

I was sitting in my room talking to God, and I told
Him that I felt like something was still holding
me, but I didn't know what it was. As clear as day,
I then heard the words, "You need to forgive her,"
and immediately I knew exactly which "her" in my
long history of hers, He was referring to. I started
trying to figure out how I would get in touch after
all these years and tell her that I was forgiving her,
but God stopped me dead in my tracks. He told
me that she didn't need to know what I was doing,
because it wasn't for her, it was for me. I had to let
go of everything she had done so that I could move
on. I sat there a little longer and just began to think
of what it really meant to forgive. What did it look
like? What did forgiving feel like? How would I know
that I had forgiven her beyond just saying the words?
Then He spoke to me again and said I didn't need to
be concerned with forgiveness having a particular
look or feeling to it. He told me that if I could get to
the point where I no longer wanted her exposed for
the things she had done to me, then I would know
that I had forgiven her. I had to release her from the
responsibility of who I had become and in turn release
myself from the hold her actions had on me. So I
began to pray that prayer and ask God to help me let
it go . . . let her go. A few days went by and again I
heard the voice of God telling me to forgive her, so
I did the only thing I could think to do at the time. I

took a page out of my closest friend's playbook and decided to use a technique she had shared with me before. I went to the store and bought a balloon, then met her at a local park. I gave her the balloon and she used one side to write down all the feelings she was experiencing that she couldn't tell anyone else. When she gave it back to me, I turned it over and wrote the woman's name and three words that everyone needs to say and hear at some point in life . . . "I forgive you". We then walked over to a bridge and I took one last look at the side I had written on. I inhaled deeply and as I exhaled, I opened my hand and released the grip that I had on the balloon. It began floating higher into the air and I stood there watching it as it became smaller and smaller in my eyes. In that moment, I knew that I was releasing more than just a balloon. I was letting go of everything that had happened to me and everything I had done. As the balloon floated away, so did my guilt and shame and it was as if a weight was lifting off of my shoulders. I had forgiven her and I was set free. I left the park that day feeling lighter, brighter and more optimistic about life than I'd ever been and I realized that all the roots had been severed. The stump was no longer connected to anything in my yard. The tedious work had paid off and now I was able to pull the stump out of the ground and cast it aside. God had given me the strength and all the tools I needed for the process and finally, the entire tree was gone.

Chapter 9

Preparing for a New Harvest

You stand back and look at your yard and breathe a sigh of relief that you've gotten rid of the pesky stump, but now you're left with a big hole that you have to deal with. Putting something new in the space may look nice, but there are still remnants of the roots that you cut and you don't want to run the risk of anything reattaching or feeding off of the same nutrients in the soil. Everything within you just wants to be done with this once and for all, so you decide to do something a little drastic. You secure the area, place wood inside the hole and set a fire to burn out the old roots and anything in the dirt that was connected to the bothersome tree. As the fire kindles, you can see it burning the wood along with the surrounding remains of the root system, until at last there are no more roots left and the wood has been completely consumed. All that you see in the hole where the massive tree once stood is ashes, and you feel a sense of accomplishment having done all that you could do to permanently free yourself of this problem. Still there is something going on in the soil that you are completely unaware of, but it is working for your benefit. The fire not only eliminated the root fragments, but it also burned out all of the organic matter in the soil and turned it into ash. It doesn't sound like a positive thing, but the ash creates a sudden burst in nutrients that can now be found in the soil. Without the fire, the nutrients would've only been released after a slow decaying process, but the result of the burning actually increases any subsequent plant growth. You have now gotten rid of all evidence of the former tree and magnified the growth potential of whatever comes next. You are ready for a new harvest!

I wish I could tell you that I didn't fall after I figured out what my root was and dug it up, but unfortunately that's not true. I had dealt with the things from the past, but I was left with a void that was still clinging to old desires and I had to burn them out. I couldn't set myself on fire in the natural sense, but there were some things I had to do spiritually to ensure that I had removed this issue from my life for good. It all started when my pastor prompted our church to go on a twenty-one day fast at the beginning of 2014. I had never fasted for that long before, but I knew that in order to get the freedom that I had never had, I had to do something I had never done. This was my chance and I took it. Prior to even getting to day one, I prayed and asked the Holy Spirit to burn out anything in me that wasn't pleasing to God and to transform me into a vessel fit for His use. I didn't know what types of changes the fast would bring, but I was excited to do anything that would get me closer to God and further away from the demons in my past. So I started making little changes that I knew I could live with and I saw God honor my commitment. Within the first week, I was already hearing God clearer and feeling His presence like never before. He was giving me specific instructions for my life and I could see the immediate manifestations as a result of my obedience. After that, I amped my fast up a bit and cut some things out of my daily routine that weren't necessarily bad, but they didn't add anything good or Godly to my life either. When I took that step, God took another step closer to me and I could feel Him working on me from the inside out. My feelings and thoughts of various people were starting to change as God changed my heart and it was even becoming evident to those around me. Friends and acquaintances were noticing a difference in my countenance and there was no way I could hide the joy I was experiencing. I was getting to know God in a way that was more personal than any other relationship I was a part of and it made me want to get even closer. By the time the last week of the fast rolled around, I had become so focused on Him that I paid no attention to my former desires and cravings and didn't even realize when they weren't an issue anymore. I just looked up one day and everything about me was different. I had done everything in my power that I knew to do and now the consuming fire of the Holy Spirit had burned through all the residue of my old life. My past was dead and all that was left was ashes. In a matter of three weeks, God had done what I tried to do in my own strength for over seventeen years. I was completely free and this time, I knew beyond a shadow of a doubt that I wouldn't go back. Out of the ashes of my former life, comes a woman that is totally dependent and totally sold out to God. I am walking in the newness of life and looking forward to the harvest that God has for me.

Now when I stand back and look at my yard, it's hard to believe that there was ever a big ugly tree located in the middle of it, but I'm glad I was able to experience it in each stage. I review the years that I spent living in sin and I am eternally thankful that I was given the chance to get things right, because now I have the opportunity to speak to the generation of people rising up that don't believe there is anything wrong with my former lifestyle. Sure, I could do like some people and bring up a bunch of scriptures to convince others of the sin nature of homosexuality, but that didn't work well when people did it to me. What I will say is that I am confident that no one chooses this lifestyle without there being some major contributing factors. It all stems from something! And if people pause long enough to really think about their situation, I'm sure they will see that there is something else attached. But that doesn't mean that anyone has to stay where they are. Everyone can have a new harvest just like me and countless others. Everyone can get to their root and dig it up just like I did. One important thing to remember is God loves us just the way we are, sin and all. But when He made us, it was in His image, and He wants us to clear out all the other roots so that we can be just like Him.

What Kind of Tree Do You Have?

I know that everyone reading this won't be able to identify with the struggle of homosexuality, but that doesn't mean you don't have a tree that needs to be dealt with. So, what does your tree look like? Is it fornication? Lying? Bitterness? Addiction? How about anger? Are you too judgmental of others? Do you harbor self-hatred? Whatever it is, it has a root somewhere. Maybe your tree is in its infancy stage and you can easily go back and pluck up the seed. Others may be at a point where you just realized that your tree is out of control and it needs to be cut down. Whichever category you fit into, God is there to help you with your next step and every one that comes after that. Your journey doesn't have to be as treacherous as mine if you are willing to commit yourself to God right here and right now, and allow Him to complete the work that He has begun in you.

My prayer for you today is that you will feel the ever present love of God as you walk through your journey. I ask our Heavenly Father to wrap His arms around you and comfort you as you get to the root of each and every issue you face. Lord, grant the strength needed to confront the difficult things in the past and let go of every hurt that may have taken place. As you make the choice to walk away from whatever is hindering your progress in God, I ask that He will dispatch His guardian angels to shield and protect you from any attack that the enemy would try to wage. You are a child of God, made in His image and likeness and you shall live in complete and total freedom. Not only will you be free, but everyone connected to you will be set free as a result of your obedience to God and transformation in God. In Jesus' Name! Amen!

Thank you for reading and I hope
you were blessed by my story.

I would love to connect with you!

Find me on Facebook: Nicole Alexander

Follow me on Twitter: @MissAlex_21

Email me: anafromtheheart@gmail.com